WRITE!

Foundations and Models for Proficiency

FOR THE STUDENT

WRITE! gives you the tools to be a better writer. You'll enjoy writing more. You may even improve your writing scores!

FOUNDATIONS

In Part I, you'll think about and practice grammar, usage, and mechanics skills. You'll also study models of various kinds of writing. And you'll do some writing of your own!

MODELS

In Part II, you'll use what you've learned in Part I as you study models of several different forms of writing. For each form of writing, you will

- see prompts and writing models.
- read partner and teacher comments on writing.
- correct errors in writing models.
- learn about rubrics, which are used to score writing.
- score some writing models on your own.
- do your own writing, with tips for help.
- work with a partner to score and improve your writing.
- make connections between writing and other parts of your life.

So, let's start to **WRITE!**

Acknowledgments

Product Development

Dale Lyle *Project Editor*

Joan Krensky *Project Editor*

Joan Talmadge *Project Editor*

Jeanine Jenks Farley *Writer*

Johanna Ehrmann *Writer*

Jo Pitkin *Writer*

Pamela Halloran *Editor*

J. A. Senn *Content Reviewer*

Design and Production

Susan Hawk *Designer/Illustrator*

Yvonne Cronin *Typesetter*

Diane Dumas *Typesetter*

ISBN 978-0-7609-2460-0

©2004—Curriculum Associates, LLC

North Billerica, MA 01862

TABLE OF CONTENTS

COMMON AND PROPER NOUNS

Whenever you write, you use nouns. A **noun** is a word that names a person, place, or thing.

Nouns such as *girl, city,* and *cookies* are called **common nouns.** They name any person, place, or thing. Nouns such as *Marie, Dallas,* and *Oat Crunch* name a particular person, place, or thing. These nouns are called **proper nouns.** Begin proper nouns with a capital letter.

	Common Nouns	**Proper Nouns**
People	brother coach	Jennifer Abraham Lincoln
Places	cabin museum	Ohio Miami Beach
Things	piano movie	Friday Big Dipper

STUDY A MODEL

Read the true story about Theodore Roosevelt. The words in red are common nouns. The words in blue are proper nouns.

As a young boy, Teddy was often sick. He spent long days in bed reading. He liked books about animals best.

Theodore Roosevelt grew up to become the twenty-sixth president of the United States. When his family lived in the White House, they had many pets. Among them were twelve horses, five bears, and a zebra. There was even a snake named Emily Spinach!

In the first sentence, the word *boy* does not name a particular person. It is a common noun. *Teddy* names a particular person. It is a proper noun and is capitalized.

Notice that the proper noun *United States* is made up of two words. Proper nouns often have more than one word. Each important word in a proper noun begins with a capital letter. Can you find three more proper nouns made up of two words?

PRACTICE

A *Match each common noun with a proper noun.*

Common Nouns	Proper Nouns
1. street	a. Dr. Lucy Watt
2. book	b. Chicago
3. city	c. Mars
4. planet	d. Saddle River Road
5. cereal	e. *Charlotte's Web*
6. dentist	f. Toasty Flakes

B *Read each sentence. Write the common noun and the proper noun that are in the sentence.*

1. We climbed Mount Wilson and walked around the lake.
2. Her birthday is in November.
3. Did Senator Goldberg visit your school yet?
4. Is Australia an island?
5. New England includes six states.
6. These paintings were done by Norman Rockwell.

C *Read the paragraph. Write the 11 common nouns. Write the 5 proper nouns.*

All over the world, people love animals. In Japan, children catch crickets and grasshoppers. They keep them in small cages made of bamboo. In Rome, the largest city in Italy, cats are especially loved. They roam all around the Colosseum and the famous buildings of the Forum.

A **common noun** names any person, place, or thing. A **proper noun** names a particular person, place, or thing. Always capitalize each important word in a proper noun.

WRITE

Write a true story about a person you know. Use exact nouns in your writing. Remember to capitalize the proper nouns.

Writing Tip

Your choice of nouns can strengthen your writing. The exact nouns in the second sentence give readers a clearer picture.

- The **girl** returned the **animal** to the **store**.
- **Mariah** returned the **gerbil** to **Pete's Pet Shop**.

PLURAL NOUNS

THINK ABOUT

Nouns can be singular or plural. A **singular noun** names **one** person, place, or thing. A **plural noun** names **two or more** people, places, or things.

There are three simple rules for making nouns plural.
- Add *s* to most nouns.
- When a noun ends in *sh, ch, s, ss,* or *x,* add *es*.
- When a noun ends in a consonant and *y,* change the *y* to *i* and add *es*.

Singular Nouns   horse, wish, sandwich, gas, glass, box, berry

Plural Nouns   hors**es**, wish**es**, sandwich**es**, gas**es**, glass**es**, box**es**, berr**ies**

STUDY A MODEL

Carlos is going to visit Adrian's home. Read the directions Adrian gave Carlos. The words in red are plural nouns.

From school, walk east for five **blocks**. After you go by a row of **stores**, turn right onto Elm Street. You will pass a park on the left with many **benches** and some tall **bushes**. Next, you will walk by two small **factories** on the right. Our apartment is in the next building, which has three **stories**. I will be waiting for you out front.

Notice that *blocks* and *stores* form their plural by adding *s*.

Because *bench* and *bush* end in *ch* and *sh*, add *es* to make them plural.

Since *factory* ends in a consonant and *y*, the *y* is changed to *i* before *es* is added. What other noun forms its plural this way?

6

PRACTICE

A *Write each underlined noun. Label it S for singular or P for plural.*

1. a brown <u>pony</u>
2. sandy <u>beaches</u>
3. colorful <u>butterflies</u>
4. the dull <u>ax</u>
5. sealed with a <u>kiss</u>
6. two leather <u>shoes</u>
7. the thick <u>bushes</u>
8. a busy <u>bee</u>

B *Read each sentence. Write the plural of the underlined noun.*

1. My sister and I washed all the <u>dish</u> last night.
2. She has two <u>dress</u> hanging in her closet.
3. Both school <u>bus</u> will arrive any minute.
4. Put all the <u>peach</u> in a basket.
5. Zaheer has pen pals in three <u>country</u>.
6. My parents pay <u>tax</u> in April.

C *Read the paragraph. Find the 11 nouns that should be plural. Write them correctly.*

Yesterday, all the boy and girls in our youth group went camping. As we were setting up the two tent, we saw three small fox. These baby crawled out from under some branch on the ground. While hiking, we found some wild blueberry and blackberry. What big mess we made as we ate these fruit! At night, we heard screech from some noisy owls. We all enjoyed the sights and sound on our camping trip.

> Add **s** to most nouns to make them **plural**. Add **es** to nouns that end in **sh, ch, s, ss,** or **x**. When nouns end in a consonant and **y**, change the **y** to **i** and add **es**.

WRITE

Write directions. Tell how to get from your home to another place. Put the steps in order so that someone can follow them easily. Write the plural nouns correctly.

Writing Tip

Using exact nouns in directions will make them easier to follow. Which direction do you think is clearer?

- Turn left at the **building**.
- Turn left at **Bunny's Bakery**.

POSSESSIVE NOUNS

THINK ABOUT

A noun sometimes changes its form to show that it owns (or is closely connected to) something else. This kind of noun is called a **possessive noun**.

To make a singular noun into a possessive noun, add an apostrophe and *s* (*'s*). When a noun is plural and ends in *s*, add only an apostrophe (') to make it possessive.

Without Possessive Nouns	**With Possessive Nouns**
the car of the *man*	the *man's* car
the color of the *sky*	the *sky's* color
the ladders of the *painters*	the *painters'* ladders
the covers of the *books*	the *books'* covers

STUDY A MODEL

Read the journal entry that Martin wrote. The words in red are singular possessive nouns. The words in blue are plural possessive nouns.

August 5
   The **sun's** rays were warm as we drove up to the **campsite's** entrance in my **uncle's** van. Just after we built a fire, a storm arrived. The rain put out the **fire's** flames. We climbed into our tents, but the wind blew open the **tents'** flaps. The **trees'** branches made a groaning sound. We spent the rest of the night in the van, looking through the **windows'** foggy glass.

 Notice that *sun's*, *campsite's*, and *uncle's* are all singular possessive nouns. All three nouns form the possessive by adding *'s*.

 The words *tents'* and *trees'* are plural possessive nouns. They form the possessive by adding just an apostrophe ('). Can you find another plural possessive noun in the journal entry?

PRACTICE

A *Write each group of words correctly by making the noun in red possessive.*

1. Maria hat
2. two boys shoes
3. a city buildings
4. three jets engines
5. a writer story
6. five readers questions
7. the book cover
8. my two sisters rooms

B *Read each sentence. Use a possessive noun to write the underlined group of words another way.*

1. The <u>chirping of the birds</u> woke us up.
2. We opened the <u>door of the van</u>.
3. The <u>web of a spider</u> sparkled in the morning dew.
4. The <u>shadows of the rocks</u> made it hard to see the chipmunks.
5. The <u>sizzling of the eggs</u> made my stomach rumble.
6. I heard <u>the voice of Uncle Dave</u> say, "Breakfast is ready."

C *Read the paragraph. Use a possessive noun to write each underlined group of words correctly.*

I enjoyed the art fair. All of the <u>students projects</u> were wonderful. <u>Sophia painting</u> had horses. The <u>horses manes</u> shone in the sunlight. <u>Pedro drawing</u> showed five airplanes in the sky. The <u>airplanes wings</u> almost touched. The <u>pilots faces</u> showed pride. I liked <u>Alexa clay dinosaurs</u> best. All of the <u>dinosaurs tails</u> were long. One <u>dinosaur long claws</u> and sharp teeth looked quite fierce.

A **possessive noun** shows who or what owns something. Add an apostrophe and **s** (**'s**) to a singular noun to make it possessive. Add only an apostrophe (**'**) to a plural noun that ends in **s**.

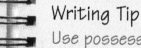

WRITE

Write a journal entry about a place or an event you would like to remember. Be sure that you form possessive nouns correctly.

Writing Tip

Use possessive nouns only to show ownership or a connection.

- The **books** are on the table. (no ownership or connection)
- The **books'** titles are listed here. (The titles belong to the books.)

PRONOUNS

Do you know what would happen if you kept repeating the same noun over and over? Your sentences would quickly become boring. A **pronoun** can take the place of one or more nouns that have just been used.

Boring: André made pancakes. André made muffins too.

Better: <u>André</u> made pancakes. **He** made muffins too.

Boring: Laura read the letter. The letter was very long.

Better: Laura read the <u>letter</u>. **It** was very long.

The pronouns *I, me, you, he, him, she, her,* and *it* take the place of singular nouns, which name one person, place, or thing.

The pronouns *we, us, you, they,* and *them* take the place of plural nouns, which name two or more people, places, or things.

STUDY A MODEL

Do you know the fable "The Tortoise and the Hare"? Read the interview a reporter had with the tortoise after the race. The words in red are pronouns.

Q: Tortoise, were you nervous before the race?

A: Yes. Hare is fast, but I never dreamed that he would take a nap.

Q: Did your friends cheer you on during the race?

A: Yes, they said that I could win it.

Q: What did Hare say to you after the race?

A: He thanked me for teaching him a lesson.

The pronoun *you* takes the place of the singular noun *Tortoise.*

The pronoun *he* takes the place of the singular noun *Hare.*

The pronoun *they* takes the place of the plural noun *friends.* What nouns do the other two pronouns in that sentence replace?

PRACTICE

A *Read each sentence. Find and write the pronoun in the sentence.*

1. I love surprises.
2. Friends gave me a surprise party last Friday.
3. The mother said to the children, "You must listen."
4. "We will follow the rules," the children replied.
5. The new puppy is soft, and it is cute too.
6. Let them feed the puppy.

B *Read each sentence. Write the noun or nouns that the underlined pronoun replaces.*

1. Ned went to the grocery store with Ella. <u>He</u> wanted to help.
2. Ella and Ned bought walnuts. <u>They</u> bought oranges too.
3. The children wondered, "Should <u>we</u> get some apples?"
4. Ned said, "Mom likes apples. Let's get <u>them</u> for Mom."
5. "Mom won't expect this," said Ella. "Won't <u>she</u> be happy!"
6. "Let <u>me</u> carry the groceries home," Ned offered.

C *Read the dialogue. Find the 10 pronouns. Write the pronouns and the nouns that they replace.*

Dad went to the baseball game. Beth and Devon went with him.

"Where will we all sit?" asked Beth.

Dad replied, "The seats for us are over there."

"Where are the players?" asked Devon. "I can't see them."

"They will be on the field soon," said Dad.

Beth asked, "May I get a hot dog with mustard on it?"

"Sure," Dad told her. "Devon, do you want a hot dog too?"

A **pronoun** takes the place of a noun. Use *I, me, you, he, him, she, her,* and *it* in place of singular nouns. Use *we, us, you, they,* and *them* in place of plural nouns.

WRITE

Write an interview between two characters from a popular story or movie. Make the interview sound like a real conversation. Be sure to use the correct pronouns.

Writing Tip

Use a pronoun only when it is clear what noun or nouns it is replacing.

- Grace and Abby are going to the movies. **She** asked Ali to go too. (Does *She* replace Grace or Abby?)
- Grace and Abby are going to the movies. **Abby** asked Ali to go too. (Now it's clear who asked Ali to go.)

PRONOUNS BEFORE AND AFTER VERBS

THINK ABOUT

Choosing the right pronouns to replace nouns is important. What pronoun to choose depends on its place in the sentence.

Use the **pronouns** *I, we, you, she, he, it,* and *they* **before verbs.**

She *kicked* the ball.

It *was* the best game ever.

We *visited* our cousins.

They *played* together.

Use the **pronouns** *me, us, you, him, her, it,* and *them* **after verbs.**

Jackie *met* **me** at school.

Tell **him** the news.

Mrs. Hill *gave* **them** a gift.

The movie *scared* **us.**

STUDY A MODEL

Read the paragraph from a story Crystal made up about her dog Hudson. The words in red are pronouns. The words in blue are verbs.

I remember when Hudson started to talk. I remind him that this special talent first appeared last summer. We were alone on the porch. He made a joke. I laughed out loud. Alyssa heard me from inside the house. She asked me what was so funny. We never told her our secret.

◀•• The first two sentences begin with the pronoun *I*, which comes <u>before</u> the verbs *remember* and *remind.*

◀•• The pronoun *She* comes before the verb *asked.* The pronoun *me* comes after the same verb. Can you find two other sentences that have a pronoun <u>before</u> and <u>after</u> the same verb?

PRACTICE

A *Decide which sentence each pronoun belongs in. Write A or B.*

| A. Cory took _____ to the movies. |
| B. _____ took Cory to the movies. |

1. I
2. us
3. me
4. she
5. they
6. her
7. them
8. we
9. him

B *Read each sentence. Write the correct pronoun to complete the sentence.*

1. Please give (I, me) the ball.
2. Throw (her, she) the Frisbee.
3. I will show (you, she) my shell collection.
4. (He, Him) went swimming yesterday.
5. Mom showed (us, we) her coin collection.
6. (They, Them) are good dogs most of the time.

C *Read the paragraphs. Write the pronouns that correctly complete the paragraphs.*

Dawn, Kevin, and Vanessa played a spooky game. First, (they, them) put on blindfolds. Then Vanessa passed (they, them) a paper bag. Kevin reached in first. (He, Him) pulled out a round, slippery object and gave it to Dawn. (She, Her) squealed and handed the object to Kevin. (He, Him) laughed and put it back in the bag.

"Can you tell (I, me) what it is, Kevin?" asked Vanessa.

"Of course (I, me) know what it is," answered Kevin.

"You gave (us, we) a peeled grape."

> Use the **pronouns** *I, we, you, she, he, it,* and *they* **before verbs**.
> Use the **pronouns** *me, us, you, him, her, it,* and *them* **after verbs**.

WRITE

Use your imagination to write a story about talking animals. Write the story so that readers will believe it. Remember to use pronouns correctly before and after verbs.

Writing Tip

In your sentences, you will sometimes use two or more pronouns together. If you have trouble choosing the right pronouns, try using one at a time.

- **Her** and **me** ran quickly. (incorrect)
- **She** ran quickly. I ran quickly. (one at a time)
- **She** and **I** ran quickly. (correct)

ACTION VERBS AND LINKING VERBS

THINK ABOUT

A sentence always has a subject and a verb. The subject tells *whom* or *what* the sentence is about. The verb is usually a word that shows action. **Action verbs** tell what the subject *does*.

Kendra **packed** a suitcase.   She **drives** a school bus.
The balloons **rose** high.   He **ironed** his shirt.

Not all verbs show action. Some connect (or link) the subject to words in the sentence that tell something about the subject. These verbs are called **linking verbs.** Forms of the verb *to be* (*am, is, are, was, were*) are common linking verbs.

I **am** tired.   Dr. Delker **was** my dentist.
A kiwi **is** a fruit.   The guests **were** late.
Fall leaves **are** colorful.

STUDY A MODEL

Read the summary of a book about the first woman to fly alone across the Atlantic Ocean. The words in red are verbs.

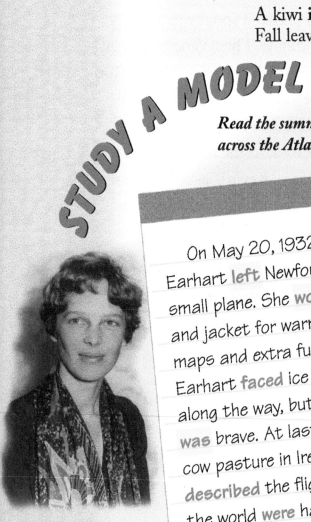

On May 20, 1932, Amelia Earhart left Newfoundland in her small plane. She wore a leather cap and jacket for warmth. She carried maps and extra fuel on board. Earhart faced ice and storms along the way, but this woman flyer was brave. At last, she landed in a cow pasture in Ireland. Newspapers described the flight. People all over the world were happy for Earhart. She was soon famous.

The words *left, wore,* and *carried* are action verbs. They tell what Amelia Earhart did.

The word *was* is a linking verb. It links the subject *flyer* to the word *brave,* which tells what the flyer is.

14

PRACTICE

A *Write the verb that best completes each sentence.*

honk	soar	sting	were	bloom	is

1. Flowers _____ in spring.
2. The music _____ loud.
3. Bees _____ sometimes.
4. Car horns _____.
5. Her toes _____ cold.
6. Hawks _____ above.

B *Read each sentence. Write the verb and label it A for action or L for linking.*

1. Mr. Marcos owns three dogs.
2. The dogs are huge.
3. He walks the dogs every morning.
4. I greet Mr. Marcos on my way to school.
5. He is always happy to see me.
6. The dogs tug at their leashes.

C *Read the paragraph. Find and write the 9 verbs. Label each verb A for action or L for linking.*

Squirrels build their nests in trees. They gather twigs and leaves for the outside of the nest. Fur and feathers are useful for the inside. Squirrels eat many kinds of food. Sometimes a lot of food is available. Squirrels store the extra food for the future. Baby squirrels arrive in the spring. The mother squirrel raises them alone. In eight to ten weeks, the babies climb out of the nest.

All sentences have **subjects** and **verbs**. An **action verb** tells what the subject *does*. A **linking verb** joins the subject to words in the sentence that tell what the subject *is*.

WRITE

Write a summary of a book you have read. Tell about only the important parts of the book. Be sure that each of your sentences has a verb.

Writing Tip

Your writing will be more powerful if you sometimes use more than one verb in a sentence.

- Tomas **made** a sandwich. He **ate** it quickly. (correct)
- Tomas **made** a sandwich and **ate** it quickly. (stronger)

15

PRESENT, PAST, AND FUTURE VERBS

You write verbs in different ways to show when the action happens. Verbs can show present, past, or future time.

A verb in the **present** shows action that **is happening now** or **happens all the time.**

➡ Brad **looks** for his book now.
My parents **surprise** me sometimes.

A verb in the **past** shows action that **has already happened.** To make most verbs show past time, add *ed*. If the verb ends in *e*, just add *d*.

➡ Yesterday Brad **looked** for his book.
My parents **surprised** me two days ago.

A verb in the **future** shows action that **will happen.** To show future time, add the word *will* before the verb.

➡ Tomorrow Brad **will look** for his book.
My parents **will surprise** me again.

STUDY A MODEL

Read the story about a boy's experience in the kitchen. The words in red are verbs.

The smell of fresh bread makes me hungry. Sometimes I bake my own bread. Yesterday I used my aunt's recipe for banana bread. This time, however, I never added the baking powder! The bread looked as flat as a pancake. My parents liked the bread anyway. Tomorrow I will visit a bakery and will buy a fresh loaf of bread.

The verb *makes* is in the present. It shows an action that happens all the time.

The verb *used* shows an action that happened in the past. The word *use* ends in *e*, so only *d* is added to show past time.

The verbs *will visit* and *will buy* show actions that will happen in the future.

PRACTICE

A *Change each verb in the present time to past time and future time.*

1. sail
2. chase
3. whistle
4. help
5. watch
6. smile
7. jump
8. clean

B *Read each sentence. Write the correct verb to complete the sentence.*

1. Tomorrow she (mailed, will mail) the letter to him.
2. A bat (will glide, glided) over my head last night.
3. The gardeners (plant, planted) seeds now.
4. Yesterday I (fix, fixed) a flat tire on my bicycle.
5. Now Eileen (paints, painted) a picture for her brother.
6. His grandparents (arrived, will arrive) next week.

C *Read the paragraph. Change each underlined verb to show the correct time.*

In 1992, Bryan Berg <u>construct</u> a 15-foot tower of cards. In 1998, he <u>need</u> only 8 days to build an 111-story tower. Many people <u>watch</u> Bryan on television. Later, Bryan built a 132-story tower. It <u>weigh</u> about 200 pounds. Bryan once <u>design</u> a 4-foot square of cards. Seventeen people <u>climb</u> on top, and the cards <u>stay</u> up! Those cards <u>support</u> about 2,700 pounds. Today, Bryan <u>make</u> card towers all over the world. Maybe he <u>visit</u> your town one day. If he comes to my town, I <u>go</u> to see him.

> Verbs can show **present, past,** or **future time.** Add **ed** to most verbs to show past time. If the verb ends in **e,** just add **d.** To show future time, add the word **will** before the verb.

WRITE

Write a story about an experience that did not turn out the way you had hoped. Remember to use the correct verb forms to show present, past, or future time.

Writing Tip

Be careful when using more than one verb in a sentence. Do not change from one time to another without a reason.

- He **raced** to the car and **jumps** into the back seat. (incorrect)
- He **raced** to the car and **jumped** into the back seat. (correct)

17

IRREGULAR VERBS

Most verbs end in *ed* or *d* to show past time. Some verbs change in special ways to show past time. They are called **irregular verbs.**

Present Time	Past Time
The show **begins** soon.	The show **began** an hour ago.
She **brings** a snack every day.	She **brought** a snack today.
The bus **comes** at eight o'clock.	The bus **came** early yesterday.
I **draw** faces well.	I **drew** her face perfectly.
I **drink** milk with every meal.	I **drank** milk with my supper.
The birds **fly** south each fall.	The birds **flew** south last fall.
He **grows** taller and taller.	He **grew** four inches in a year.
We **hear** a noise right now.	We **heard** a noise a minute ago.
I **keep** secrets well.	I **kept** a secret for many weeks.
You **know** a lot about cars.	You once **knew** a lot about cars.
I **make** my bed in the morning.	I **made** my bed early this morning.
We **see** a rainbow now.	We **saw** a rainbow earlier.
I **think** about my pet every day.	I **thought** about my pet yesterday.

STUDY A MODEL

Read the true story about cocoa. The words in red are irregular verbs.

In the 1500s, the Spanish explorer Cortés **came** to Mexico. He **saw** that the people there **grew** cocoa beans. Cortés **drank** their special cocoa drink. He **thought** it tasted bitter. He **brought** some cocoa beans back to Spain. There he **made** a sweeter drink with the beans. The Spanish **kept** the recipe a secret for many years. In time, people all over Europe **heard** about the sweet cocoa drink.

The verb *come* changes its first vowel to form the verb *came* in the past. Find two other irregular verbs that form past time by changing one vowel.

The verb *think* changes several letters to form the verb *thought* in the past. Find another irregular verb that ends in the same way as *thought,* to show past time.

The verb *hear* changes by adding the letter *d* to form the verb *heard* in the past.

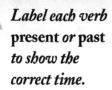

PRACTICE

A *Label each verb present or past to show the correct time.*

1. come
2. flew
3. keep
4. brought
5. grow
6. know
7. drank
8. see
9. began

B *Read each sentence. Change the underlined verb to show past time.*

1. Yesterday I <u>draw</u> a picture.
2. I <u>know</u> it was a good drawing.
3. I <u>think</u> of a good title for it.
4. I <u>keep</u> the drawing on my desk.
5. Then I <u>hear</u> about an art show.
6. I <u>bring</u> my drawing to the art show.

C *Read the paragraphs. Change each underlined verb to show past time.*

When she was nine years old, Margaret Knight <u>begin</u> a job in a cotton mill. In the 1800s, many children worked in such factories. One day, a piece of steel <u>fly</u> out of the loom. Several children <u>see</u> the steel hit a worker. Margaret <u>hear</u> about this accident. She <u>think</u> about it a great deal. Then she <u>know</u> what to do. She <u>make</u> a device so this wouldn't happen again.

Later, she <u>draw</u> plans for another invention. It was a machine that produced grocery bags with square bottoms. Have you ever <u>bring</u> these bags home from a store?

Irregular verbs change in special ways to show past time.

WRITE

Write a true story about the first time you tasted a food you had never eaten before. What did you think of this food? Watch out for irregular verbs in your writing.

Writing Tip
Keep a list of irregular verbs that cause you trouble. Some can be put in groups.

bring/brought   blow/blew   creep/crept
buy/bought   draw/drew   keep/kept
fight/fought   fly/flew   sleep/slept
think/thought   grow/grew   sweep/swept
  know/knew   weep/wept
  throw/threw

MAIN VERBS AND HELPING VERBS

THINK ABOUT

Some sentences you write will have a verb that is used alone. In other sentences, a **helping verb** comes before a **main verb**.

Eric **mows** the lawn once a week. (The verb is used alone.)
Eric **is mowing** the lawn now. (The first verb is the helping verb. The second verb is the main verb.)

Most Common Helping Verbs
am, is, are, was, were, have, has, had, will, can, may

The verbs *am, is, are, was, were, have, has,* and *had* can each be used alone. Each verb can also be used as a helping verb before a main verb.

Verb Alone
I **am** sleepy.
She **has** long hair.

Helping Verb Before a Main Verb
I **am writing** a poem.
She **has seen** that movie.

STUDY A MODEL

Read the story about a girl's promise. The words in red are helping verbs. The words in blue are single verbs or main verbs.

It was Saturday. Erin Nelson loved Saturdays. Her father was making pancakes. After breakfast, Erin was going to the baseball field with her friends. But Erin's mother had other ideas for her.

"Have you cleaned your room, Erin?" Mrs. Nelson asked.

Erin's friends were waiting for her. Quickly, Erin shoved clothes under her bed. Then she bolted out the door with a promise to her mother. "I will finish later. You can count on it!"

In the first sentence, the verb *was* is used alone. In the third sentence, *was* is the helping verb, and *making* is the main verb.

In most sentences, the helping verb and main verb are together. This sentence is a question. Here, the subject *you* comes between the helping verb *have* and the main verb *cleaned*.

PRACTICE

A *Label each underlined verb H for helping verb or M for main verb.*

1. am <u>working</u>
2. were <u>playing</u>
3. <u>has</u> tried
4. will <u>eat</u>
5. <u>was</u> grinning
6. <u>are</u> jumping
7. <u>is</u> crying
8. will <u>run</u>

B *Read each sentence. Write the helping verb that is used with the underlined main verb.*

1. We are <u>studying</u> for the big test.
2. Alejandra is <u>helping</u> me.
3. I was <u>worried</u> earlier about failing.
4. We had <u>hoped</u> to be done studying by now.
5. Has your noisy brother <u>left</u> the apartment yet?
6. I am <u>expecting</u> to do well on the test now.

C *Read the paragraphs. Write the verb that goes with each underlined subject. If the verb is more than one word, circle the helping verb.*

<u>George Washington Carver</u> was once a slave. In 1864, <u>Carver and his mother</u> were kidnapped. <u>Carver</u> was still a baby, and <u>he</u> was returned. Sadly his <u>mother</u> disappeared forever.

In 1891, <u>Carver</u> studied at Iowa State College. <u>He</u> was the school's first African-American student. <u>Carver</u> became a plant scientist. <u>He</u> taught people about the many uses of peanuts. <u>You</u> can thank Dr. Carver for the invention of over 325 peanut products.

Verbs can be used alone or with helping verbs. The verbs *am, is, are, was, were, have, has,* and *had* can each be used alone or as a **helping verb** with a **main verb**.

WRITE

Write a story about a promise that you made to someone or that someone made to you. Be sure that you use verbs correctly.

Writing Tip

When writing a sentence, you usually want to put the subject first. This makes the sentence more active. Be careful about putting the subject last. This can make the sentence unclear and dull.

- The pitcher **threw** the ball. (clear and strong)
- The ball **was thrown** by the pitcher. (Here the helping verb *was* isn't helping at all!)

SUBJECT-VERB AGREEMENT

THINK ABOUT

In every sentence you write, the **subject** and the **verb** should **agree**. They must both be either singular or plural.

Use a singular verb when the subject is a singular noun or the pronoun *he*, *she*, or *it*. There are three rules for making verbs singular.

- Add *s* to most verbs.
- Add *es* to verbs that end in *ch, sh, ss, x,* or *z.*
- When a verb ends in a consonant and *y,* change the *y* to *i* and add *es.*

Use a plural verb when the subject is a plural noun or the pronoun *I, we, you,* or *they.* No ending is added to a plural verb.

Subjects	Verbs	Sentences
Grace	live + *s*	Grace **lives** nearby.
she	teach + *es*	She **teaches** fifth grade.
eagle	fly − *y* + *i* + *es*	The eagle **flies** overhead.
they	splash	They **splash** in the water.

STUDY A MODEL

Read the description of an everyday event. The words in red are subjects. The words in blue are verbs.

Sometimes Ben Cohen drives to work. But usually he rides the bus. It passes by his street. Each morning, Ben dashes out the door and down the street. He crosses the busy street at the corner. Ben hurries to catch the bus. Most of the time, he misses it. The passengers watch him. They wave to him. Ben waits patiently for the next bus.

Because the subject *Ben Cohen* is singular, an *s* is added to *drive* to make it singular too.

The verb *crosses* is singular because the subject *He* is singular. An *es* is added to *cross* because it ends in *ss.*

The singular verb *hurries* agrees with the singular subject *Ben.* The *y* in *hurry* is changed to *i* before adding *es.*

The plural verb *watch* has no ending. It agrees with the plural subject *passengers.*

PRACTICE

A *Write each verb correctly to complete the sentence.*

Sometimes Desi _____.

1. whistle	4. study	7. relax
2. fish	5. guess	8. worry
3. march	6. cry	9. listen

B *Read each sentence. Write the underlined verb correctly so that it agrees with the subject.*

1. Grandpa <u>fry</u> eggs for us each morning.
2. Lang never <u>miss</u> the bus.
3. The cereal <u>crunch</u> in my mouth.
4. They <u>finish</u> their chores quickly each day.
5. Elena <u>mix</u> the cake batter.
6. Leaves <u>float</u> on the water.

C *Read the paragraph. Write each underlined verb correctly so that it agrees with the subject.*

Aza <u>search</u> for ideas on how to take good photographs. She <u>study</u> other people's work. On clear days, the sun <u>make</u> dark shadows on faces. So Aza <u>watch</u> the sky for clouds. Aza <u>divide</u> a photograph into thirds in her mind. Then she <u>fix</u> the shot by putting the subject on one of the lines. Next, Aza <u>get</u> in close. Sometimes she <u>try</u> to photograph only the person's head and shoulders.

A subject and its verb must agree. When the subject is singular, add **s** to most verbs. Add **es** to verbs that end in **ch, sh, ss, x,** or **z.** When a verb ends in a consonant and **y,** change the **y** to **i** and add **es.** When the subject is plural, do not add an ending to the verb.

WRITE

Write a description of someone or something that you have seen in your town or city. Be sure that each verb agrees with its subject.

Writing Tip

The subject of a sentence sometimes has more than one noun or pronoun. If you don't know what verb to use, think of a pronoun that can take the place of the subject. This will help you choose the correct verb.

- Gwen and Will (**like/likes**) pizza.
  They
- <s>Gwen and Will</s> **like** pizza.

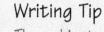

23

MORE SUBJECT-VERB AGREEMENT

THINK ABOUT

The verbs *am, is, are, was,* and *were* are all forms of the verb *to be.* Be sure you choose the form of the verb *to be* that agrees with the subject.

Use *am* and *was* with the pronoun *I.*

I **am** not sleepy now.   I **was** sleepy earlier.

Use *is* and *was* with a singular noun or the pronoun *he, she,* or *it*.

Her coat **is** too long.   **Was** it waterproof?

Use *are* and *were* with a plural noun or the pronoun *we, you,* or *they.*

Are the eggs fresh?   You **were** late again.

STUDY A MODEL

Read the true story about the rescue of a baby sea otter.
The words in red are subjects. The words in blue are verbs.

I am a rescue worker for the zoo. My job is fun, but it is not always easy. Several months ago, an otter was lost at sea. Goldie was only several weeks old at the time. Young otters are helpless without their mother. For a while, zookeepers were Goldie's "mom." They were Goldie's pals and teachers too. Finally, Goldie was strong. She is now on her own in the sea. Are you happy for her?

The verb *am* agrees with the pronoun *I.*

The verb *was* agrees with the singular noun *otter.*

Notice that the pronoun *you* comes after the verb *Are.* In questions, the subject often follows the verb. To be sure the subject and verb in a question agree, make the question a statement, by putting the subject first: *You are happy for her.*

PRACTICE

A *Read each sentence. Write the verb that agrees with the underlined subject.*

1. Right now <u>they</u> (is, are) in the lunchroom.
2. <u>She</u> (is, are) an excellent kickball player.
3. <u>I</u> (am, is) a good painter.
4. Hot <u>soup</u> (is, are) wonderful on a cold day.
5. <u>We</u> (am, are) cousins.
6. (Am, Is) the <u>book</u> enjoyable?

B *Read each sentence. Write the correct verb to complete the sentence.*

1. Yesterday (was, were) a wonderful day.
2. I (was, were) at a park with my friends.
3. We (was, were) there to celebrate Eduardo's birthday.
4. The weather (was, were) perfect.
5. No clouds (was, were) in the sky.
6. My friends (was, were) happy to see me.

C *Read the paragraph. Write the verbs that correctly complete the paragraph.*

I (am, are) curious about tomatoes. Did you know that the tomato (is, are) not a vegetable? Tomatoes (is, are) fruits because they contain seeds in the part of the plant that is eaten. For a long time, many people (was, were) not willing to eat tomatoes. They grew tomatoes because they thought the plant (was, were) pretty. Today, tomatoes (am, are) the third largest crop in the United States.

> Use the verbs **am** and **was** with the pronoun *I.* Use **is** and **was** with a singular noun or the pronoun **he, she,** or **it**. Use **are** and **were** with a plural noun or the pronoun **we, you,** or **they.**

WRITE

Write a true story about a time when you helped someone or when someone helped you. Be sure that the subjects and verbs in your sentences agree.

Writing Tip

Subject-verb agreement can be tricky. Be sure you know what noun the verb should agree with.

- The dishes on the shelf (**is/are**) clean.

The writer is talking about the clean dishes, not the clean shelf. **Dishes** is a plural noun, so the verb should be **are**.

25

EXACT VERBS

Using **exact verbs** can make your sentences stronger and more lively. Exact verbs give readers a better picture of what is taking place.

Read these sentences. See how the use of exact verbs creates a clear picture in your mind.

The cook **stepped** out of the kitchen.
The cook **stumbled** out of the kitchen.
The cook **stormed** out of the kitchen.

Exact verbs *show*, rather than *tell*, what is happening.

Alex was in a hurry to catch his bus, so he quickly made a sandwich.

Alex **slapped** some cheese between two slices of bread and **bolted** out the door to catch his bus.

Notice how the verbs in the second sentence *show* that Alex was in a hurry.

STUDY A MODEL

Read the description of Katrin's cat. The words in red are verbs.

Most of the time, Missy struts around with her tail in the air. When she spots her toy mouse, she twitches her whiskers and waves her tail. Then she pounces on the mouse. Loud noises frighten Missy. She tucks her tail between her legs and hisses. At night, Missy and I cuddle on the sofa. Missy curls into a ball on my lap. I stroke her fur, and she purrs like a little engine.

The verbs *struts, spots, twitches, waves,* and *pounces* are strong action words. They help you picture exactly what Missy is doing.

The verb *hisses* makes a sound effect. The word sounds like what it means. Can you find another verb in Katrin's description that makes a sound effect?

PRACTICE

A *Match each verb with a more exact verb.*

1. cry
2. said
3. wrote
4. ate
5. laugh
6. see

a. yelled
b. gobbled
c. giggle
d. gaze
e. whimper
f. scribbled

B *Read each sentence. Write the verb that is more exact.*

1. We (strolled, walked) through the park.
2. The baseball (went, whizzed) into the outfield.
3. A squirrel (runs, scurries) across the branches.
4. I (scraped, took) the mud off my shoes.
5. A rabbit (scampered, went) into a hole.
6. The thirsty child (drank, gulped) a glass of lemonade.

C *Read the paragraph. Write a more exact verb for each underlined verb.*

I <u>looked</u> out the window one wintry morning.
Two feet of snow <u>covered</u> our yard! I <u>went</u> outside.
My feet <u>moved</u> across the ice on our steps. I almost <u>fell</u>
to the ground. The cold air <u>hurt</u> my cheeks, and
I <u>touched</u> them with my gloves. I <u>made</u> a snow wall.
I hid behind the wall as my friend Jane <u>walked</u> near.
Then I <u>got</u> up and surprised her.

Use **exact verbs** to give readers a clearer picture of what is taking place.

WRITE

Write a description of a person or an animal. Try to use exact verbs in your description.

Writing Tip
Use a thesaurus to find exact verbs for your writing. A thesaurus is a special kind of dictionary. It contains words and their synonyms. (Synonyms are words that have the same or almost the same meaning.)

ADJECTIVES

An **adjective** is a word that describes a noun. Adjectives give color to your writing.

An adjective can come before or after the word it describes.

He wore a **blue** jacket. *(adjective before noun)*
His jacket was **blue**. *(adjective after noun)*

An adjective can tell *what kind, how many,* or *which one.*

The clothes are **dirty**. *(what kind)*
He read **three** books. *(how many)*
I will buy **these** shoes. *(which one)*

The words *a, an,* and *the* are a special kind of adjective. They are called *articles.* These three small words come before many nouns.

STUDY A MODEL

Read the recipe for making cheese pizza. The words in red are adjectives. The words in blue are the nouns that the adjectives describe.

This recipe is easy. Just follow these directions. The first step is to stretch the dough into a big circle. Shape a small rim around the edge. Next, spread a spicy red sauce on top. Then sprinkle the top with several types of cheese. Bake the pizza in a hot oven for ten minutes or until the crust is crisp. Slice the pizza into eight pieces and enjoy.

In the first sentence, an adjective comes before and after the noun *recipe.* The adjective *This* tells *which one,* and the adjective *easy* tells *what kind.*

Notice that two adjectives, *spicy* and *red,* appear before the noun *sauce.* Together, these adjectives give readers a clear idea of what the sauce is like.

The adjective *several* tells how many. Can you find two more adjectives that tell how many?

PRACTICE

A *Write the adjective that describes each underlined noun. Do not include articles.*

1. flying kites on windy <u>days</u>
2. tasted the salty <u>popcorn</u>
3. under a leafy <u>tree</u>
4. cheesy <u>crackers</u> for a snack
5. those <u>beetles</u> on the leaf
6. bitten by several <u>wasps</u>
7. three <u>days</u> from now
8. stepped on a rusty <u>nail</u>

B *Read each sentence. Write the adjective. Do not include articles.*

1. Many animals live in the ocean.
2. The claws of a crab are strong.
3. The octopus has eight legs.
4. Lobsters are found on the eastern coast.
5. Do you think that sharks are scary?
6. Most sharks do not harm people.

C *Read the paragraph. Find and write the 12 adjectives. Then write the noun that each adjective describes. Do not include articles.*

Abraham Lincoln's childhood was unusual. He was born in Kentucky in a small cabin made of logs. His entire family moved seven years later. Their new home was in Indiana. Lincoln's stepmother was kind. She thought he was a good boy. Lincoln seldom went to school, but he was an eager learner. He read and reread the few books his family owned. As a young man, Lincoln had many jobs. He also had big dreams.

> An **adjective** describes a noun by telling *what kind, how many,* or *which one.*

WRITE

Write a set of directions telling how to do something. Be sure the steps are in the correct order. Use adjectives to help make your directions clear to readers.

Writing Tip
Use *a* before words that begin with a consonant sound. Use *an* before words that begin with a vowel sound.
- A gorilla is **an** ape.
- **An** elephant has **a** trunk.

ADJECTIVES THAT COMPARE

You can use adjectives to compare. To compare two people, places, or things, add *er* to the adjective. To compare three or more people, places, or things, add *est*. When an adjective is long, put the word *more* or *most* before it rather than adding *er* or *est*.

The knife is **sharp.**
This knife is **sharper** than that knife.
This is the **sharpest** knife of all.

The test was **difficult.**
This test was **more difficult** than yesterday's test.
This was the **most difficult** test this year.

Some adjectives change spelling when they are used to compare.

- If an adjective ends in a single vowel and consonant, double the consonant and add *er* or *est*. *(sad, sadder, saddest)*
- If an adjective ends in a silent *e*, drop the *e* and add *er* or *est*. *(white, whiter, whitest)*
- If an adjective ends in a consonant and *y*, change the *y* to *i* and add *er* or *est*. *(dry, drier, driest)*

STUDY A MODEL

Read the opinion that Luis has written about a pet. The words in red are adjectives that compare.

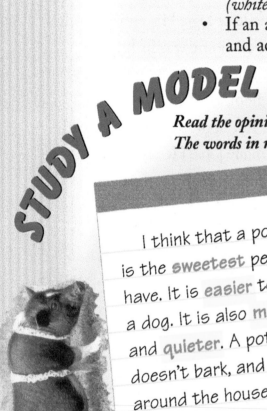

I think that a pot-bellied pig is the sweetest pet anyone can have. It is easier to care for than a dog. It is also more intelligent and quieter. A pot-bellied pig doesn't bark, and it doesn't run around the house. Yes, a dog is thinner than a pot-bellied pig, and often cuter. But in my mind, a pot-bellied pig is the most lovable pet of all.

The adjective *easy* ends in a consonant and *y*, so *y* is changed to *i* before *er* is added.

The adjective *intelligent* is long, so the word *more* is used to compare the two animals. The adjective *quiet* is a short word, so *er* is added.

The word *thin* ends in a single vowel and consonant, so the consonant is doubled before *er* is added. The word *cute* ends in silent *e*, so the *e* is dropped before *er* is added.

PRACTICE

A *Change the adjectives in Group A to compare two. Change the adjectives in Group B to compare three or more.*

Group A
1. tall
2. calmest
3. green
4. most colorful

Group B
5. brown
6. more interesting
7. high
8. sweeter

B *Read each sentence. Write the underlined adjective correctly by adding the ending.*

1. July is usually the <u>hot</u> winter month. (*est*)
2. My parents are <u>wise</u> than I. (*er*)
3. She is the <u>friendly</u> person I ever met. (*est*)
4. He has the <u>red</u> hair in his family. (*est*)
5. Anna's joke was <u>funny</u> than mine. (*er*)
6. I am <u>happy</u> today than I was yesterday. (*er*)

C *Read the paragraphs. Write the underlined adjectives correctly.*

Jesse Owens was the <u>speedy</u> runner in his high school. In 1935, he also made the <u>long</u> jumps at track events. At the 1936 Olympic games, Owens was the <u>fast</u> runner in the races he took part in. His records lasted 20 years!

Chuck Yeager set one of the <u>exciting</u> records of all. He flew an airplane <u>fast</u> than the speed of sound.

Was either of these two men <u>successful</u> than the other?

Add **er** or the word **more** to adjectives when comparing two people, places, or things. When comparing three or more people, places, or things, add **est** or the word **most**.

WRITE

Write your opinion about something that you feel strongly about. If you use adjectives that compare, be sure to spell them correctly.

Writing Tip
The adjectives *good* and *bad* change in special ways when used to compare.

Adjective	Compares Two	Compares Three or More
good	better	best
bad	worse	worst

EXACT ADJECTIVES

Try to avoid using common adjectives when you are describing a noun. More **exact adjectives** give readers a clearer picture of the person, place, or thing.

The **hot** soup tasted **good**. → The **steaming** soup tasted **delicious**.

THINK ABOUT

Adjectives	More Exact Adjectives
bad	dangerous, evil, naughty, poor, terrible, wicked
big	enormous, gigantic, huge, immense, mammoth, tall
cold	chilly, cool, crisp, freezing, frosty, icy, nippy, wintry
good	correct, delicious, enjoyable, honest, loyal, useful
great	excellent, famous, glorious, magnificent, wonderful
hot	boiling, burning, fiery, sizzling, spicy, steaming
little	miniature, short, slender, slight, slim, small, tiny
nice	charming, helpful, kind, pleasant, polite, sweet
old	aged, ancient, antique, elderly, primitive, stale, worn

STUDY A MODEL

Read the paragraph about a boy and his little brother. The words in red are exact adjectives. They replace common adjectives.

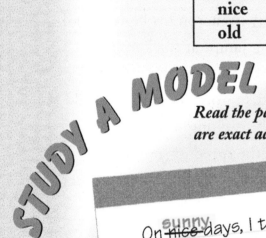

On ~~nice~~ sunny days, I take William for a ~~little~~ short walk. Today we watched an ~~a big~~ enormous power shovel knock down ~~an old~~ a crumbling building. William said the power shovel looked like a ~~bad~~ dangerous monster. When the air got ~~cold~~ chilly, we came home. We read ~~a good~~ an enjoyable book called Mike Mulligan and His Steam Shovel. William and I had a ~~great~~ wonderful day together.

The word *nice* is common. The adjective *sunny* better describes the day.

Notice how the adjective *crumbling* gives a clearer picture than the word *old*.

The word *good* is so common that it adds very little to a noun's meaning. Replacing *good* with a stronger adjective, like *enjoyable,* makes the meaning clearer.

PRACTICE

A *Match each underlined adjective with a more exact adjective.*

1. <u>hot</u> soup
2. <u>cold</u> water
3. <u>good</u> work
4. a <u>bad</u> fall
5. a <u>nice</u> kitten
6. a <u>little</u> bead

  a. freezing
  b. terrible
  c. sweet
  d. boiling
  e. correct
  f. tiny

B *Read each sentence. Write the more exact adjective.*

1. Rory is a (loyal, good) friend.
2. Is the taco sauce (hot, spicy)?
3. The painter did a (bad, sloppy) job.
4. The (mammoth, big) elephant snorted and stomped.
5. It's time to replace those (old, worn) sneakers.
6. Here's a (frosty, cold) glass of lemonade.

C *Read the paragraph. Write a more exact adjective for each underlined adjective.*

When the weather is <u>hot</u>, I like to cool off in the lake. Then I sit under a <u>big</u> tree in the shade. In the winter, when it is <u>cold</u>, I like to sled or skate. I'm <u>good</u> at sledding and always have a <u>great</u> time. I'm a <u>bad</u> skater and fall down often. The <u>little</u> skating rink near my house is a <u>nice</u> place to meet friends.

Use **exact adjectives** to give readers a clearer picture of what you are describing.

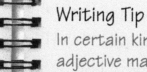

WRITE

Write a paragraph about something that you have seen while walking or riding your bike in your neighborhood. Be sure to use exact adjectives.

Writing Tip

In certain kinds of writing, a common adjective may be exactly what you need to make a point. Short sayings such as the following can sometimes create the perfect effect:

- Good work!
- Nice job!
- Great idea!

ADVERBS

You can make your sentences more interesting and clear by using adverbs. An **adverb** is a word that describes a verb. Adverbs can come *before* or *after* the verbs they describe. Many adverbs end in *ly*.

Read these two sentences. See how the adverbs in the second sentence give you a clearer picture of what is happening.

I walked onto the stage and looked at the audience.

I **slowly** <u>walked</u> onto the stage and <u>looked</u> **nervously** at the audience.

An adverb can describe a verb by telling *how*, *when*, or *where*.

Rufus barks **loudly**. *(how)*
Rufus barks **often**. *(when)*
Rufus barks **outside**. *(where)*

STUDY A MODEL

Read the description that Casey wrote about playing baseball.
The words in red are adverbs.

I never miss a baseball game. Often I arrive early. We had an exciting game yesterday. In the last inning, I stood at the plate and firmly gripped the bat. Then I waited calmly for the right pitch. On the third pitch, I hit the ball sharply. It sailed high over the fence. My teammates cheered loudly. Excitedly I rounded the bases. I want to play baseball forever.

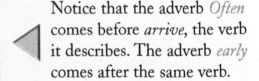

Notice that the adverb *Often* comes before *arrive*, the verb it describes. The adverb *early* comes after the same verb.

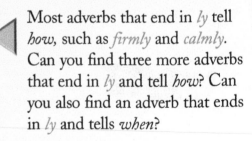

Most adverbs that end in *ly* tell *how*, such as *firmly* and *calmly*. Can you find three more adverbs that end in *ly* and tell *how*? Can you also find an adverb that ends in *ly* and tells *when*?

PRACTICE

A *Write the 6 adverbs that could complete this sentence.*

| The football fans cheered _____. |

wildly	someday	again
backward	outdoors	loudly
suddenly	excitedly	neatly

B *Read each pair of sentences. Only the adverbs are different in each pair. Write the adverbs.*

1. Natalie happily rode her bike.
   Natalie slowly rode her bike.
2. The guests arrived early.
   The guests arrived late.
3. The bird flies above.
   The bird flies nearby.
4. Darius neatly put away his clothes.
   Darius hurriedly put away his clothes.

C *Read the paragraph. Write the 11 underlined adverbs. Label each one How, When, or Where.*

Rain is water that falls from clouds <u>overhead</u>. The rain cycle begins in the ocean. Ocean water rises <u>unseen</u> in the air. These water droplets are very small. You could not <u>easily</u> see them. <u>Next</u>, the small water droplets combine. They <u>slowly</u> form larger drops. These drops are <u>now</u> too heavy to stay in the air. They fall <u>quickly</u> to the earth as rain. The raindrops <u>quietly</u> make their way to rivers and streams. The rivers and streams run <u>downhill</u> into the ocean. <u>Soon</u> the rain cycle begins <u>again</u>.

> An **adverb** is a word that describes a verb by telling *how, when,* or *where.*

WRITE

Write a description of something that you do well. Use adverbs to make your writing clear.

Writing Tip
Be careful not to confuse *good* and *well.* *Good* is an adjective, and *well* is usually an adverb.

- Rachel is a *good* dancer. (The adjective *good* describes the noun *dancer.*)
- Rachel can sing *well* too. (The adverb *well* describes the verb *sing.*)

HOMOPHONES

THINK ABOUT

Some words can be confusing because they sound the same. Words that sound alike but have different meanings and spellings are called **homophones**.

for/four	We waited **for** the plane over **four** hours.
hear/here	I **hear** that a library is being built **here**.
its/it's	The oak tree lost **its** leaves, and now **it's** bare.
knew/new	Destiny already **knew** the **new** girl in class.
threw/through	Jake **threw** a ball **through** the window.
your/you're	**You're** going to like **your** new neighbors.

You need to learn the correct homophones to use in your writing. There are no spelling rules to help you remember them.

STUDY A MODEL

Read the article about shoes. The words in red are homophones.

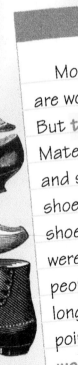

Most people know that shoes are worn to protect their feet. But they're worn for fashion too. Materials such as wood, leather, and silk have been used to make shoes. At first, there were no left shoes or right shoes. Both shoes were the same. Around 1400, people began to wear shoes with long, pointed toes. Some had points nearly two feet long! Where would you see these shoes today?

 They're is a contraction of the words *they are*. If you substitute these two words in the sentence, they make sense. This helps you know that *they're* is the correct homophone, not *there* or *their*.

The words *wear* and *Where* form a homophone pair. Find two other homophone pairs in the article.

The number word *two* is a homophone of *to* and *too*. Can you think of any other number words that have homophone partners?

PRACTICE

A *Match each word to its meaning.*

1. wood
2. four
3. threw
4. it's
5. here
6. wear

a. tossed
b. a material that comes from trees
c. the contraction of *it is*
d. a nearby place
e. to put on
f. the number that comes after *three*

B *Read each sentence. Write the word that correctly completes the sentence.*

1. The twins are over (there, their).
2. (Their, They're) names are Josh and Ian.
3. They went (to, two) the park.
4. I like to play kickball (to, too).
5. (Your, You're) a good friend.
6. I like (your, you're) shoes.

C *Read the paragraph. Write the underlined words correctly.*

Do you <u>no</u> any inventors? <u>There</u> people like you and me. Did you ever <u>here</u> of 14-year-old Becky Schroeder? Her idea <u>four</u> an invention was to put glow-in-the-dark paint on paper. She put writing paper over the painted paper. Then she could write in the dark! Becky <u>new</u> she had a good idea. <u>Its</u> an invention used by many today. Doctors use it <u>too</u> read patients' charts at night. Astronauts use the invention <u>to</u>. They use it to read when <u>they're</u> lights are turned off.

Homophones are words that sound alike but have different meanings and spellings.

WRITE

Write an article about the clothes you like to wear. Try to include as many homophones as you can in your article.

Writing Tip

In your writing journal, keep a list of homophones that you have trouble spelling. Write the homophones in sentences so that you can tell the words apart.

KINDS OF SENTENCES

THINK ABOUT

Writing is made up of sentences. A **sentence** is a group of words that tells a complete thought. Every sentence begins with a capital letter and ends with a punctuation mark. There are four kinds of sentences.

A **statement** tells something. It ends with a period (.). → The crowd cheered the runners.

A **command** tells someone to do something. It ends with a period (.). → Please open the window.

A **question** asks something. It ends with a question mark (?). → Did Nadia arrive yet?

An **exclamation** shows strong feeling. It ends with an exclamation point (!). → That was a wonderful movie!

STUDY A MODEL

Read the travel ad. Notice the different kinds of sentences the writer used. The end punctuation is red.

Are you looking for adventure? Join us on a coast-to-coast trip aboard the Breeze. Our train has many modern features. Its glass roof allows you to see the splendid scenery. Gaze at pine forests, mountains, and clear blue lakes. Can you think of a better way to see our beautiful country? Don't delay. Call today. We'd love to have you all aboard!

This sentence is a command. The subject of a command is understood to be the word *you.* Can you find the three other commands in the ad?

This sentence is a statement that tells about the train's glass roof.

This sentence asks a question, so it ends with a question mark.

The exclamation point at the end of the last sentence lets readers know that the words should be read with excitement.

PRACTICE

A *Read each sentence. Label it S for statement, Q for question, C for command, or E for exclamation.*

1. Wave to Emma.
2. Where are you going?
3. What time is it?
4. Don't do that.
5. What a huge box that is!
6. I like to ride my bike.
7. The sunset is so colorful!
8. Our house is yellow.

B *Read each sentence. Add a period, a question mark, or an exclamation point to the end.*

1. I hit my finger with the hammer
2. Are you hurt
3. No, I'm all right
4. Be careful next time
5. What are you doing
6. What a great birdhouse you built

C *Read the paragraph. End each sentence with the correct punctuation mark.*

(1) What do you know about the U.S. flag   (2) Each of the original 13 colonies had its own flag   (3) George Washington raised the first U.S. flag   (4) When did this happen   (5) It happened way back in 1776   (6) That was such an exciting event   (7) Where did it happen   (8) It happened in Cambridge, Massachusetts   (9) Always treat the flag with respect   (10) Do not drag it on the ground (11) I think the flag is a marvelous symbol of our nation

A **sentence** tells a complete thought. **Statements** tell something. **Questions** ask something. **Commands** tell someone to do something. **Exclamations** show strong feeling.

WRITE

Write a travel ad. Make readers want to go to the place you are describing. Try to include all four kinds of sentences in the ad.

Writing Tip

In a command, the subject is not stated. The subject is understood to be you. You are the person being told or asked to do something.

- (You) Sit still.
- (You) Have a safe trip.

SENTENCE FRAGMENTS

THINK ABOUT

A **sentence fragment** is a group of words that does not tell a complete thought. Often a fragment begins with a capital letter and ends with a punctuation mark. It looks like a sentence, but it is only part of one.

You can correct a sentence fragment by adding words. The fragment may be missing a subject, a verb, or both.

Am tired of the heat. ⟶ I am tired of the heat. (subject added)

The dog in the grass. ⟶ The dog rolls in the grass. (verb added)

In the deep blue sea. ⟶ Dolphins swam in the deep blue sea. (subject and verb added)

You can also correct a sentence fragment by joining it to a sentence that comes before or after.

The frog jumped. Into the pond. ⟶ The frog jumped into the pond.

After dinner. We watched TV. ⟶ After dinner we watched TV.

STUDY A MODEL

Read the first draft of an announcement that Stella wrote. The words in red are sentence fragments. Then read the announcement with the fragments corrected.

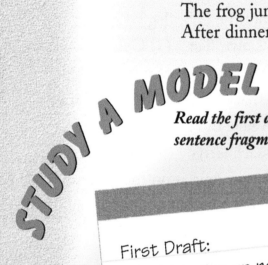

First Draft:
Everyone sign up now for the science fair. At the Gott School. The fair on March 6. This is your chance to find answers. To your questions. May have fun too!

Final Copy:
Everyone sign up now for the science fair at the Gott School. The fair is on March 6. This is your chance to find answers to your questions. You may have fun too!

This fragment does not tell a complete thought. Stella corrected the fragment by joining it to the sentence that came before it.

This fragment is missing a verb. The verb *is* completes the thought.

The last fragment needs a subject to tell a complete thought. The missing subject is *You.*

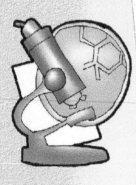

PRACTICE

A *Read each group of words. Label it* **S** *for sentence or* **F** *for fragment.*

1. Anteaters eat mostly ants and termites.
2. Can eat 30,000 ants and termites a day.
3. Anteaters in forests and on grassy plains.
4. Anteaters live in Central and South America.
5. No teeth but a sticky tongue about two feet long.
6. An anteater licks up insects with its long tongue.

B *Find the sentence fragment in each pair. Correct the fragment by joining it to the complete sentence. Write the new sentence.*

1. The giant anteater is the largest anteater.
2. At six feet long.

3. The silky anteater is a small animal.
4. With soft yellow or gray fur.

5. When in danger.
6. An anteater will roll itself into a ball.

C *Read the paragraph. Find the 10 sentence fragments. Write the paragraph correctly.*

Aardvarks are like anteaters. In many ways. But they are not related. Aardvarks live in Africa. Feed mostly on ants and termites. Aardvarks about four to six feet long. A long tail and a long snout. Aardvarks can dig a deep tunnel. Within a few minutes. Their very sharp claws. Can easily tear open insects' nests. Their tongues long and sticky. Lick up insects quickly. Aardvarks are also called earth pigs. And ant bears.

A **sentence fragment** is a group of words that does not tell a complete thought. It is only part of a sentence.

WRITE

Write an announcement for a real or made-up event at your school. Make your readers want to attend the event. Be sure that your announcement does not contain sentence fragments.

Writing Tip

If you are unsure about whether you have written a sentence fragment, ask yourself questions. *Who did this? What did this? What happened?*

- Went to the store.
  (Who went to the store?)
- In the produce aisle.
  (What happened in the produce aisle?)

JOINING SENTENCES

Sometimes your writing will read more smoothly if you combine two short sentences into one.

Use the word **and** to join two sentences that show connected ideas.

> Izzy is making lunch. Abe is helping him.
> Izzy is making lunch, **and** Abe is helping him.

Use the word **but** to join two sentences that show a difference or a problem.

> We wanted a picnic. It started to rain.
> We wanted a picnic, **but** it started to rain.

Always use a comma (,) before **and** or **but** when joining sentences.

STUDY A MODEL

Read the journal entry written by a girl who was disappointed.
*Notice the sentences that are joined by **and** or **but**.*

April 25
   Yesterday was my birthday, but my party was today. Aunt Lucy gave me a gift, and I opened it eagerly. The gift was a big, fuzzy sweater, and it looked enormous. It could fit both my sister and me together! I was disappointed, but I didn't want Aunt Lucy to feel bad. I thanked her for the gift, and she smiled.

The first sentence combined two sentences that showed a difference. This is why the word *but* joins the sentences. Notice the comma (,) before *but*.

The third sentence uses the word *and* to join two sentences that showed connected ideas. Notice the comma (,) before *and*.

PRACTICE

A *Read each sentence. Write the numbers of the 5 sentences that were made by joining two shorter sentences.*

1. Mom cooked the eggs, and I made the toast.
2. Everyone but Rishi arrived on time for the concert.
3. My hands were cold, but I left my mittens at home.
4. The wind blew, and the trees swayed.
5. Alicia looks a lot like her brother and sister.
6. The rain stopped, but it was too dark to go outside.
7. The hiker was thirsty, and her leg muscles were sore.

B *Read each pair of sentences. Use a comma and the word **and** or **but** to join the sentences.*

1. Dana carried the ball. I carried the bat.
2. Leif fell. He did not hurt himself.
3. Willard told a joke. Olga laughed.
4. I dropped the groceries. All the eggs cracked.
5. Foxes have fluffy tails. Beavers have flat tails.
6. I called. No one heard me.

C *Read the paragraph. Join the underlined pairs of sentences with a comma and the word **and** or **but**.*

(1) Bats are mammals. They fly like birds. (2) Some people think that bats have feathers. They don't. A bat's body is furry. (3) Bats hunt at night. They sleep during the day. Bats hang upside down to sleep. (4) Most bats eat insects or fruit. Some eat fish or small animals. (5) Some bats live alone. Many bats live with thousands of other bats.

> Use the word **and** or **but** to join two short sentences into one sentence.
> When joining sentences, always use a comma (,) before **and** or **but**.

WRITE

Write a journal entry about a time when you were disappointed. Describe what happened to make you feel that way and what you did after that. Watch for short sentences that can be joined with <u>and</u> or <u>but</u>.

Writing Tip

If you want to call attention to a particular sentence, don't join it with another one.

- I ran out the door and down the street, but I still missed the bus! (correct.)
- I ran out the door and down the street. Still, I missed the bus! (much stronger)

RUN-ON SENTENCES

THINK ABOUT

When you write, your ideas sometimes come quickly and run together. Sentences that are too long can be hard to understand. Break these **run-on sentences** into shorter sentences.

One kind of run-on sentence has two or more complete thoughts with no punctuation to separate them.

We dug a hole then we planted the apple tree. (*run-on sentence*)
We dug a hole. Then we planted the apple tree. (*correct*)

The other kind of run-on sentence has too many complete thoughts joined by the word *and*.

Our cat chased a squirrel up a tree and she climbed onto a high branch and now she can't get down. (*run-on sentence*)

Our cat chased a squirrel up a tree. She climbed onto a high branch. Now she can't get down. (*correct*)

STUDY A MODEL

Read the first draft that Todd wrote. It has many run-on sentences. Then read his final copy.

First Draft:
    My room is in the attic I share the room with my brother, Jason. He and I have bunk beds and he sleeps on the bottom bunk and I sleep on the top bunk.

Final Copy:
    My room is in the attic. I share the room with my brother, Jason. He and I have bunk beds. He sleeps on the bottom bunk. I sleep on the top bunk.

In the first sentence, two complete thoughts run together without any mark of punctuation. When Todd broke the run-on sentence into two sentences, the meaning became clearer.

The second run-on sentence had three complete thoughts joined by the word *and*. This long sentence was hard to understand. Todd corrected it by breaking it into three shorter sentences.

PRACTICE

A *Read each sentence. Label it C for correct or R for run-on.*

1. Tali was hiking in the woods she saw a fox.
2. For breakfast I ate cereal. I ate a sandwich for lunch.
3. In an hour the play starts you must be ready.
4. I walked in the park. A dog crossed my path.
5. The sand was hot. It burned my feet. I ran to the water.
6. The boy read awhile and then he turned off his lamp and at last he fell asleep.

B *Read each run-on sentence. Break the sentence into shorter sentences.*

1. It is winter I like to go sledding on snowy days.
2. The first snow fell last night I watched out the window.
3. The ground was white six inches of snow had fallen.
4. I pulled on my boots and I put on my hat and gloves and then I raced outside.
5. I shoveled the walk and then I ran to the park and there my friends and I went sledding.

C *Read the paragraph. Find the three run-on sentences. Write each one as shorter sentences.*

People all over the world eat rice Americans eat about 25 pounds of rice each year. In parts of Asia, people eat 400 pounds of rice each year. Rice is important and popular and it has been a common food for a long time. People grew rice 4,000 years ago. In the 1600s, rice was brought to the American colonies it soon became a major crop.

> A **run-on sentence** may have two or more complete thoughts with no punctuation to separate them. It may also have too many complete thoughts joined by the word *and*. Break all run-on sentences into shorter sentences.

WRITE

Write a description of a room in your home. When you are done, read your description. Are all of your sentences clear? Did you write any run-on sentences?

Writing Tip

To check for run-on sentences, always read aloud what you have written. Or, have someone else read your writing. You may sometimes miss mistakes that another person can find easily.

CAPITALIZATION

As you write, remember to **capitalize** certain words.

Capitalize the **first word** of a sentence.	My job is to feed the dog.
Capitalize the pronoun *I*.	My brother and **I** are twins.
Capitalize the **names** and **initials** of people.	The letter came from **E**lle **M**. **W**ong.
Capitalize **titles** used with people's names.	Vote for **M**ayor **P**at **K**aufman.
Capitalize the names of **special places**.	Is **T**own **H**all in **N**orthfield on **M**ain **S**treet?

THINK ABOUT

STUDY A MODEL

Read the news article. The words in red begin with a capital letter.

BIG BASS PLACES FIRST

Pleasant Lake, Washington

The winner of this year's fishing derby is Amy Maggio, a student at Collins Middle School. Her catch was a six-pound bass.

Amy's uncle, Dr. Paul R. Caruso, taught her how to fish. "My first fishing pole was a gift from Uncle Paul," said Amy. "My uncle and I love to fish together."

Notice that each word in *Collins Middle School* begins with a capital letter. Always capitalize the complete names of special places, except for small words, such as *for, of, the,* or *by*.

In the third sentence, the word *uncle* is not capitalized because it is used alone.

In the fourth sentence, *Uncle* is capitalized because it is a title used with the name *Paul*.

PRACTICE

A *Write each name and place correctly. Use capital letters.*

1. cedar Street
2. Mrs. agnes Smith
3. boise, idaho
4. dr. Katarina Alvarez
5. Arun n. Madhu
6. Mount everest
7. columbia River
8. Fire chief Jack Moore

B *Read each sentence. Find the word that should be capitalized. Write that word correctly.*

1. Yesterday i went to the store.
2. Julia is my cousin from michigan.
3. My pen pal, Gil, lives in Sydney, australia.
4. My family went to San francisco.
5. We strolled through golden Gate Park.
6. the Transamerica Building looks like a pyramid.

C *Read the paragraph. Find the 10 words that should be capitalized. Write those words correctly.*

my family just moved. Now we live on S.W. salmon Street in Portland, Oregon. Before we moved to Portland, we lived in seattle. My parents, andrew and Tessa Monroe, like our new home. dad got a job here in town. At dinner yesterday, I met his boss, dr. w. Chan. My new school is Creekside elementary School. Yesterday i made my first friend. Her name is Cassie lee.

> Always **capitalize** the **first word** of a sentence. Also capitalize the pronoun *I*, people's **names** and **initials**, and **titles** used with people's names. Capitalize the names of **special places** too.

WRITE

Write a news article about something that has recently happened to you or someone you know. Remember that a news story answers the five Ws: who, what, when, where, and why. Be sure to capitalize all important words.

Writing Tip

Capitalize such words as *mother, father,* and *grandma* only when you use them as names.

- Did you ask **Grandpa** to join us? (*Grandpa* is used as a name.)
- Did you ask your **grandpa** to join us? (Here *grandpa* is not used as a name.)

MORE CAPITALIZATION

THINK ABOUT

As you write, remember to **capitalize** the names of **special things**.

Capitalize the names of **days**.	Sunday, Wednesday
Capitalize the names of **months**.	December, April
Capitalize the names of **holidays**.	Memorial Day, Labor Day
Capitalize the names of **pets**.	Snowball, Goldie
Capitalize the **titles** of stories, poems, books, and magazines.*	"The Golden Goose" (story), "Trees" (poem), *The Wind in the Willows* (book), *Newsweek* (magazine)

*Capitalize the first word, the last word, and each important word in titles. Do not capitalize *a, an, and, by, for, in, of, the,* or *to* unless it is the first or last word.

STUDY A MODEL

Read the description of a family's new pet. The words in red are the capitalized names of special things.

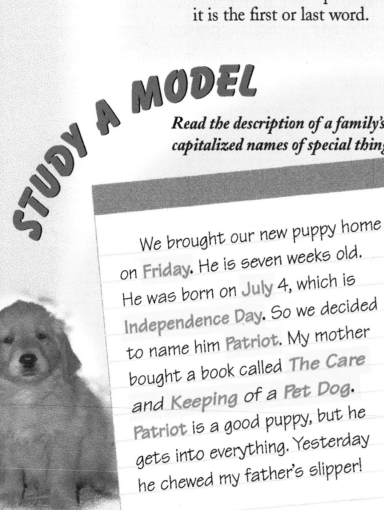

We brought our new puppy home on Friday. He is seven weeks old. He was born on July 4, which is Independence Day. So we decided to name him Patriot. My mother bought a book called *The Care and Keeping of a Pet Dog.* Patriot is a good puppy, but he gets into everything. Yesterday he chewed my father's slipper!

Notice that the names of the day, the month, and the holiday each begin with a capital letter.

The word *Patriot* begins with a capital letter because it names the family pet.

The word *the* is not usually capitalized in a title, but it is here because it is the first word in the title.

PRACTICE

A *Find each name of a special thing. Write that name correctly.*

1. next wednesday
2. the fable "the ant and the grasshopper"
3. last august
4. every thanksgiving
5. my hamster clem
6. the book *meet my pet giraffe*

B *Read each sentence. Find the name of a special thing. Write that name correctly.*

1. George Washington was born on february 22, 1732.
2. Presidents Washington and Lincoln are honored on presidents' day.
3. This holiday is always celebrated on a monday.
4. George Washington owned a parrot named polly.
5. Have you read the book *washington and the revolution*?
6. I wrote a poem called "our first president."

C *Read the paragraph. Find the 8 names of special things. Write the names correctly.*

Alan Alexander Milne was born january 18, 1882. Today he is better known as A. A. Milne. Milne wrote the book *winnie-the-pooh*. In this book a young boy solves problems with the help of his toy pets. Their names are pooh, tigger, eeyore, and piglet. Milne's books are still very popular. This saturday, I will buy my little brother the book *now we are six*. I might also get him a jar of honey.

> **Capitalize** the names of **special things,** such as days, months, holidays, and pets. Also capitalize each important word in titles of stories, poems, books, and magazines.

WRITE

Write a description of a pet. The pet can be real or make-believe. Tell how the pet behaves and what foods it eats. In your description, remember to capitalize the names of special things.

Writing Tip

When you are using a computer to write, use *italics* for titles of books, magazines, TV programs, and movies. <u>Underline</u> these titles when you are writing by hand. Use "quotation marks" for titles of stories, poems, and songs.

COMMAS

A **comma** (,) is used in a sentence to signal a pause or to separate words and ideas.

Use a **comma** after the words *yes, no, well,* and *oh* when they begin a sentence.

Yes, I will come with you.   Well, where should we go?

Use a **comma** to separate the name of a person being spoken to from the rest of a sentence.

Amber, can you help me?   I will dry the dishes, Louis.

Use a **comma** after each word, *except* the last word, in a series of three or more.

Ryan, Arturo, and Drew are late.   Buy milk, flour, and bread.

STUDY A MODEL

Read the interview between a teacher and his students.
The commas are red.

Mr. Eads: Rob, what is your project
  with Ari, Jada, and Molly?

Rob: We are studying lizards, sharks,
  spiders, and starfish.

Mr. Eads: Oh, what do these animals
  have in common?

Jada: Well, all of them can grow
  new body parts.

Ari: Did you know that lizards can grow
  a new tail, Mr. Eads?

Molly: Yes, and sharks are always
  growing new teeth.

In this sentence, Mr. Eads is calling Rob by name. A comma separates the student's name from the rest of the sentence.

Notice that there is a comma after each word in the series, except the last word (*starfish*).

A comma is used after *Well,* because it begins the sentence. Can you find two other words used in this way that are also followed by a comma?

PRACTICE

A *Read each sentence. A comma is needed after one word in the sentence. Write that word and the comma.*

1. Pia do you know what pets our presidents owned?
2. No tell me about them.
3. Well there were so many that it's hard to begin.
4. Just tell about the most popular pets Deb.
5. Oh those would be dogs and cats.
6. Yes that's what I thought.

B *Read each sentence. Commas are needed after 2 or more words in the sentence. Write those words and the commas.*

1. James Garfield owned a horse a dog and several fish.
2. Sheep chickens and cats were Woodrow Wilson's pets.
3. Abraham Lincoln owned a turkey a goat and a rabbit.
4. Lincoln also owned cats dogs pigs and ponies.
5. Andrew Jackson had three horses whose names were Truxton Emily and Bolivia.
6. Theodore Roosevelt owned twelve horses five bears a zebra and a snake.

C *Read the paragraph. Find the 11 words that should be followed by a comma. Then write the paragraph correctly.*

Was President Calvin Coolidge a pet lover? Yes he was. He had three canaries whose names were Nip Tuck and Snowflake. Oh he also had three cats whose names were Bounder Tiger and Blacky. Coolidge owned a donkey a bobcat and a bear. Well that's not all. He also had an antelope a wallaby and a lion.

Use a **comma** (,) to signal a pause or to separate words and ideas.

WRITE

Write an interview that includes several people. Have them talk about a group of things or people that are connected somehow. Be sure to use commas correctly.

Writing Tip
If you are not sure where to put commas, read your writing to yourself. Listen to where you pause. This is probably where a comma should go.

APOSTROPHES IN CONTRACTIONS

THINK ABOUT

A **contraction** is a shortened word made by joining two words. An **apostrophe** (') takes the place of any letters that are left out.

When you talk, you use contractions a lot. For example, you could say, "**We are** going to school, and **she is** going too." However, you are more likely to say, "**We're** going to school, and **she's** going too."

Some contractions are formed by joining a verb and the word *not*. Other contractions are formed by joining a pronoun and a verb.

Verb + *not*	Contraction	Pronoun + verb	Contraction
are + not	aren't	it + is	it's
did + not	didn't	he + would	he'd
do + not	don't	you + are	you're
have + not	haven't	they + are	they're
was + not	wasn't	you + will	you'll
were + not	weren't	we + will	we'll

STUDY A MODEL

Read the description that Kelly wrote about her friend.
The words in red are contractions.

I couldn't ask for a better friend than Velma! She's smart, funny, and kind to others. She won't leave anyone out. If I'm upset, she'll listen to me and cheer me up. Velma isn't perfect. Sometimes she's in a bad mood. However, she usually doesn't stay that way for long. I'd rather spend time with Velma than with anyone else. I can't think of a better friend.

The contraction *couldn't* is made by joining the verb *could* and the word *not*. The apostrophe replaces the letter *o* in *not*.

The contraction *won't* is irregular. It is made by joining the verb *will* and the word *not*.

The contraction *I'd* is made by joining the pronoun *I* and the verb *would*. When a pronoun is joined with a verb, only the verb is shortened. The spelling of the pronoun stays the same.

PRACTICE

A *Match each contraction with the words that were joined to make it.*

1. weren't
2. you'll
3. doesn't
4. I'm
5. aren't
6. they're

a. are not
b. were not
c. I am
d. does not
e. you will
f. they are

B *Read each sentence. Write the underlined contraction correctly.*

1. <u>Didnt</u> you hear me?
2. <u>Its</u> time to go.
3. <u>Well</u> need to hurry.
4. We <u>dont</u> want to be late.
5. <u>Isnt</u> Phil coming?
6. <u>Hed</u> like to, but he has to study.

C *Read the e-mail message. Write the underlined words as contractions.*

Lucy,

  <u>I am</u> excited about seeing you again. We <u>have not</u> seen each other in a long time. <u>I would</u> like to see you more often. <u>You are</u> my favorite cousin. It <u>will not</u> be long before the weekend is here. <u>We will</u> probably see a mystery one night. <u>It is</u> my favorite type of movie. I think <u>you will</u> like the mystery too.

Ruby

A **contraction** is a shortened word made by joining a verb and another word.
An **apostrophe** (') takes the place of the letter or letters that are left out.

WRITE

Describe a friend. He or she can be a friend you have or a friend that you would like to have. Use contractions in your description.

Writing Tip

Don't confuse contractions with their homophones. If you are not sure whether to use a contraction in a sentence, say the contraction as two words. If the two words sound correct, then the contraction is correct.

  It's (It is) time to give the lion **its** dinner.
  You're (You are) carrying **your** backpack.

QUOTATIONS IN DIALOGUE

THINK ABOUT

A conversation between two people or more is called **dialogue**. The speakers' words are called **quotations**. As you write dialogue, be sure to capitalize and punctuate the quotations properly.

- Surround a speaker's *exact words* with **quotation marks** (" ").
  "You look as if you need help," the librarian said.

- **Capitalize** the *first word* of a *quotation*.
  Jesse replied, "Yes, I'm looking for a good mystery."

- Use a **comma** (,) to separate a *quotation* from the words that *name the speaker*.
  "I can recommend several mysteries," the librarian told him.

- Use a **punctuation mark** *after the last word* of a quotation but *before the quotation mark*.
  Jesse exclaimed, "That's great!"

STUDY A MODEL

***Read the jokes that Kyle and Amanda are telling.
Notice the capital letters and punctuation marks.***

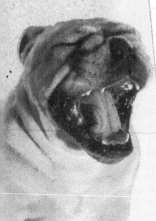

Kyle asked, "Why did the puppy go to jail?"

"I have no idea," said Mandy.

Kyle exclaimed, "It was barking in a No Barking zone!"

"I have a joke for you," said Mandy. She smiled and asked, "What kind of stories do puppies like best?"

Kyle replied, "That's a tough one. What kind?"

"They like furry tales," Mandy answered.

In the first sentence, a comma separates the quotation from the words that tell who the speaker is. (Quotation marks do not go around these words.) The word *Why* is capitalized because it is the first word of the quotation.

A quotation can come before or after the words that name the speaker. In both cases, the speaker's exact words are followed by a punctuation mark and surrounded by quotation marks.

PRACTICE

A *Read each sentence. Write the sentence correctly using quotation marks.*

1. Jessica asked, What kind of sandwich do you have?
2. Sara replied, I have a cheese sandwich.
3. I have a tuna sandwich, said Jessica.
4. Jessica added, I have an apple too.
5. I'll trade my orange for your apple, suggested Sara.
6. Yes, I'll trade, Jessica agreed.

B *Read each sentence. Each one is missing a capital letter, a comma, or end punctuation. Write the sentence correctly.*

1. Miles asked, "what are you looking for?"
2. Juanita asked, "What time is it"
3. "Let's eat" Deirdre suggested.
4. Kaitlin said, "It's hot outside"
5. "let's go swimming," Gabe suggested.
6. Amar shouted, "That's a great idea"

C *Read the dialogue. Find the sentences in which capitalization or punctuation is missing. Write those sentences correctly.*

Haley and Nate were waiting at the bus stop. It's cold today complained Haley.

Nate rubbed his hands together to warm them up. I can see my breath, he said.

Haley asked, where's the bus? She stomped her feet angrily.

Nate looked up the street for the bus. He was so cold.

He grumbled What a day to be late!

Always surround a speaker's *exact words* with **quotation marks** (" "). **Capitalize** the *first word* of a *quotation.* Use a **comma** (,) to separate a *quotation* from the words that *name the speaker.* Use a **punctuation mark** *after the last word* of a quotation but *before the quotation mark.*

WRITE

Write a dialogue between two people telling each other jokes. Look over your dialogue when you are done. Be sure you have capitalized and punctuated the quotations correctly.

Writing Tip

Remember to use quotation marks only for words that are actually spoken.

- Mrs. Gale asked Luis, "Why are you late for school?"
- Mrs. Gale asked Luis why he was late for school. (no quotation marks needed)

PARAGRAPHS

A piece of writing is usually made up of paragraphs. A **paragraph** is a group of sentences about **one main idea**.

Each time you present a new idea, you should begin a new paragraph. The first line of each paragraph is moved in a few spaces, or **indented**.

> Cecil Booth had a problem to solve. He liked to keep things clean, but he didn't like to work hard. In time, he invented the vacuum cleaner. It was so big that it took two men to run it.
>
> For many years, vacuum cleaners were sold door-to-door. A salesman would spill dirt all over a customer's carpet. Then the salesman would show how well the vacuum worked.

STUDY A MODEL

Read the two paragraphs about a famous children's author. Notice that each paragraph is indented.

Dr. Seuss faced a big challenge. His publisher wanted him to write a children's book using only a short list of words. The list had no adjectives. It took Dr. Seuss a year to write *The Cat in the Hat*, but it was soon a huge hit.

Several years later, Dr. Seuss wrote *Green Eggs and Ham*. After that, Dr. Seuss was often served green eggs and ham at the places he visited.

◄ The first sentence tells readers what the paragraph is going to be about. The rest of the sentences explain what the challenge was.

◄ The writer started a new paragraph because the main idea changed. The second paragraph is about another book that Dr. Seuss wrote. Notice that the words *Several years later* provide a bridge. They help readers move smoothly from one paragraph to the next.

PRACTICE

A *Read each sentence. Write the numbers of the 4 sentences that could go in a paragraph about the main idea.*

Main idea: <u>A computer has many uses</u>.

1. You can write letters, reports, or stories with a computer.
2. You can also use a computer to store information.
3. You can use a computer to search the Internet.
4. You can find books about computers in the library.
5. You can use a computer to play games, draw, or hear music.

B *Read the paragraph. Write the numbers of the 6 sentences that tell about the underlined main idea.*

<u>Life was very different one hundred years ago</u>. (1) Back then, people did not drive cars. (2) They did not have computers. (3) They did not have TVs or telephones. (4) Our family has a new TV. (5) There was not even electricity! (6) A hundred years ago, most people worked on farms. (7) They worked hard all day. (8) Today many people work in business offices.

C *Read the paragraph. Write a paragraph that includes the 5 sentences that tell about the underlined main idea.*

<u>Mom and Dad told me what life was like when they were my age</u>. (1) They did not have computers. (2) They wrote most things by hand or used a typewriter. (3) My grandparents still own my mom's old typewriter. (4) My parents did not have VCRs or DVD players. (5) They saw movies only at the theater. (6) There were also no cell phones when Mom and Dad were young. (7) My older brother has his own cell phone.

A **paragraph** is a group of sentences about **one main idea**.
Always **indent** the first line of each new paragraph.

WRITE

Write about a book that you enjoyed reading when you were younger. Remember to indent a paragraph that starts a new idea.

Writing Tip

In dialogue, begin a new paragraph each time the speaker changes.

　　Darla heard a loud knock on the door and called out, "Who is it?"

　　"I have a package for you," a stranger's voice answered.

　　"Thank you," replied Darla. "Just leave it on my doorstep."

MAIN IDEA AND DETAILS

Every paragraph should have a **main idea**. The main idea tells what the paragraph is mostly about. A paragraph should also have **detail sentences,** which tell more about the main idea.

main idea   detail sentences

Long ago, every village had a town crier. This person would walk through the village and call out the news. Frequently the news was days old.

main idea   detail sentences

Reporting the news is much different today. Now we can just turn on our radio or TV to hear the news. We often learn about events as they happen.

In both paragraphs, the first sentence states the main idea. The main idea is often found in the first or last sentence of a paragraph.

STUDY A MODEL

Read the article about the important work of firefighters. Look for the main idea of each paragraph.

Firefighters face great danger in their job. Sometimes they go into burning buildings to rescue people. They have to watch for falling objects. They have to be careful about breathing in smoke or getting too close to the heat. Firefighters do more than put out fires. They teach people about fire dangers in the home. They also check that buildings meet safety laws.

◀•• The main idea of this paragraph is the danger that firefighters face. The detail sentences explain some of the dangers.

◀•• The main idea of this paragraph is the other jobs that firefighters do. The detail sentences tell about those jobs.

PRACTICE

A *Read the paragraph. Write the numbers of the 3 detail sentences that tell about the underlined main idea.*

<u>In the 1200s, people in England began to use last names</u>. (1) The last name often had to do with a job. (2) If your name was William and you worked as a cook, you became William Cook. (3) My last name is Miller. (4) A man named Thomas who cut hair would be Thomas Barber.

B *Read the paragraph. Write the sentence that best completes it. The sentence should be a detail about the underlined main idea.*

<u>Many last names came from people's jobs</u>. A smith was someone who worked with metal. A cooper made wooden barrels. A carter drove an ox-cart that carried goods.

1. Some people used two last names.
2. What job do you think someone named Fisher had?

C *Read the paragraph. Write a new paragraph that includes the 4 sentences that tell about the underlined main idea.*

<u>Not all last names came from England</u>. (1) Rodriguez is a Spanish name. (2) Vogel is a German name. (3) I like learning about the history of words. (4) Okuda is Japanese. (5) What language is your last name from? (6) Many words in English come from other languages.

Every paragraph should have a **main idea** and **detail sentences**. The main idea tells what the paragraph is mostly about. The detail sentences tell more about the main idea.

WRITE

Write an article about a job. Tell why you think it is important. Begin a new paragraph each time you state a new main idea. Be sure that the detail sentences tell about the main idea.

Writing Tip

After you have written a paragraph, reread it. Ask yourself, "Is the main idea clear? Will readers understand what I am saying? Do all of my details support the main idea? Do I have enough details?"

VARYING SENTENCES IN PARAGRAPHS

THINK ABOUT

Your writing will grab your readers' attention better if you vary your sentences. One way to vary sentences is to begin them in different ways.

These three sentences all begin with the pronoun *I*.

I wanted to buy a funny birthday card for Uncle Joel. **I** went to the store after school. **I** finally found the right card.

By changing the way the sentences start, the writing becomes more lively.

I wanted to buy a funny birthday card for Uncle Joel. **After school,** I went to the store. **Finally,** I found the right card.

STUDY A MODEL

Read about the discovery of a product that is used every day. Notice how the sentences begin in different ways.

One day in 1948, George de Mestral and his dog walked through some weedy fields. When they got home, George noticed something unusual. Burrs from plants were stuck to his pants and his dog's fur. George examined the burrs under a microscope. The burrs had hooks on the ends. This gave George an idea. He worked on his idea eight years. At last, George de Mestral invented Velcro!

The writer introduces the first sentence with words that tell the time of the action. Can you find two more sentences that begin with time words?

George is the subject of several sentences in this paragraph. However, his name begins only this sentence. To keep readers interested, the writer varied the way the sentences start.

PRACTICE

A *Read the paragraphs. Write the number of the paragraph in which the sentences vary.*

1.   Coins are made from round discs called blanks. The blanks are heated to soften them. They are washed and dried to make them shiny. The blanks are then sorted to get rid of any blanks that are the wrong shape. The blanks go through a machine that puts a rim on them. The blanks are finally stamped with a design.

2.   Coins are made from round discs called blanks. First, the blanks are heated to soften them. Then the blanks are washed and dried to make them shiny. To get rid of any blanks that are the wrong shape, the blanks are sorted. Next, the blanks go through a machine that puts a rim on them. Finally, the blanks are stamped with a design.

B *Read the paragraph. Write the number of the sentence that best completes the paragraph because it varies from other sentences.*

The U.S. Mint uses long strips of metal to make coins. Each metal strip is 1,500 feet long. First, workers put each metal strip into a machine. Then a press punches round discs out of the strip. The round discs are called blanks.

1. The round discs will be made into coins.
2. Soon the round discs will be made into coins.

C *Read the paragraph. Rewrite it so that the sentences begin differently.*

A person using a magnifying glass checks coins that are newly stamped. A machine then counts the new coins. The machine drops the coins into bags next. The bags are sewn shut. The bags are eventually put on forklifts and placed in vaults. The bags are taken to banks last.

> To make your writing more lively, **vary** the way your **sentences** begin.

WRITE

Describe a product that you use every day. How does it make your life easier? Remember to vary the way the sentences start in your description.

Writing Tip

Another way to add variety to your writing is to include some long sentences and some short sentences. Join two short sentences into a longer sentence when needed. You also can break a long sentence into two shorter sentences.

PROOFREADING

Always check your writing for mistakes. Finding and correcting mistakes in written work is called **proofreading**.

You can use the marks below to show what changes should be made in your writing. These marks are known as **proofreading symbols**.

Proofreading Symbols	Meanings	Examples
≡	Change a small letter to a capital letter.	capitalize the first letter.
/	Change a capital letter to a small letter.	Make a S̸mall L̸etter.
¶	Begin a new paragraph.	Writing stories is fun. ¶ Start a new paragraph when the main idea changes.
℘	Take out this letter, word, punctuation mark, or sentence. It is not needed.	Take out any exxtra letters, misspelled words, or incorrect punctuation, marks. Also take out this sentence.
∧	Add a missing letter or word.	Put in ∧one or more words or letter∧s.
⊙	Add a period.	This is the end ⊙
⌄	Add a comma.	Put a comma here ⌄ Kim.
∨	Add an apostrophe.	Adam∨s sentence is missing an apostrophe.
⧉ ⧉	Add quotation marks.	⧉Put the quotation marks here,⧉ the writer said.

Here's how one writer marked changes in a paragraph.

¶ Yesterday I took my niece Jordan to the zoo. It was Jordan's
first visit, and she loved it. Near the entrance too the zoo, we
saw a big tortoise and a red parrot. In the ape house, chimps were
playing with one another. Young Monkeys were climbing in the
branchs. they played noisily. "I had a great day, Jordan said to
me when we finally left.

**Read this paragraph. It has 10 mistakes. Use the proofreading symbols to mark
the changes that should be made.**

I saw a TV show about one womans trip to East africa. On the
first day, she saw lions One mother lion had two small cubs.
Next, the woman seen elephants. They flapping their ears.
"Elephants flap their ears to keep cool, the woman explained.
Last, the woman saw Zebras. Zebras look like striped horses
but they cant be tamed like horses.

Now write the paragraph correctly. Make the changes you marked above.

_____

_____

_____

_____

_____

_____

Read the story about a group of people who came to America hundreds of years ago. Then answer questions 1–18.

The Pilgrims' Journey

(1) On september 6, 1620, a group of people boarded a tiny ship called the *Mayflower*. (2) They left their homes in England to go far away to a new land. (3) These people were later called Pilgrims.

(4) The journey across the Atlantic Ocean was bad. (5) The ship was very crowded. (6) The *Mayflower* was made of wood. (7) Most of the time, the Pilgrims stayed below deck, where it was cold and dark. (8) The passengers wore the same clothes nearly the whole time. (9) And their was no place to take a bath.

(10) Winter storms arrives after many days at sea. (11) Winds howled. (12) Huge waves crashed across the deck. (13) The passengers were wet cold and seasick. (14) They were afraid that the ship would sink. (15) But the *Mayflower* stayed afloat. (16) On November 9, a sailor high up on the ships mast spotted something. (17) He cried out, "land ho!" (18) It had been 66 days since the Pilgrims had seen land. (19) Them were tired and nearly out of food.

(20) The *Mayflower* anchored off the coast of what is now massachusetts. (21) The Pilgrims' long journey were over. (22) Shouted with joy to be leaving the crowded ship.

(23) The Pilgrims knowed very little about their new world. (24) They searched for a place to settle they decided on Plymouth.

(25) Life on the *Mayflower* had been hard, but life in Plymouth was even difficulter. (26) The first winter was long and cold. (27) But when the *Mayflower* returned to England in the spring, no Pilgrims were aboard. (28) They were in their new home to stay.

1. What change should be made in sentence 1?
   Ⓐ Change *september* to *September.*
   Ⓑ Change *group* to *groups.*
   Ⓒ Change *called* to *call.*
   Ⓓ Change *Mayflower* to *mayflower.*

2. The meaning of sentence 2 would be made clearer by changing *go* to
   Ⓐ *be.*
   Ⓑ *went.*
   Ⓒ *sail.*
   Ⓓ *look.*

3. The meaning of sentence 4 would be made clearer by changing *bad* to
   Ⓐ *not good.*
   Ⓑ *difficult.*
   Ⓒ *easy.*
   Ⓓ *fun.*

4. Which detail sentence does not belong in the second paragraph?
   Ⓐ sentence 5
   Ⓑ sentence 6
   Ⓒ sentence 7
   Ⓓ sentence 8

5. What change should be made in sentence 9?
   Ⓐ Change *their* to *there.*
   Ⓑ Change *no* to *know.*
   Ⓒ Change *to* to *two.*
   Ⓓ Make no change.

6. What change should be made in sentence 10?
   Ⓐ Change *storms* to *storm.*
   Ⓑ Change *arrives* to *arrived.*
   Ⓒ Change *days* to *day.*
   Ⓓ Change *days* to *day's.*

7. How can sentences 11 and 12 best be combined?
   Ⓐ Winds howled, but huge waves crashed across the deck.
   Ⓑ Winds howled, huge waves crashed across the deck.
   Ⓒ Winds howled. and huge waves crashed across the deck.
   Ⓓ Winds howled, and huge waves crashed across the deck.

8. In sentence 13, *wet cold and seasick* should be changed to
   Ⓐ *wet, cold, and seasick,*
   Ⓑ *wet, cold, and, seasick.*
   Ⓒ *wet cold, and seasick.*
   Ⓓ *wet, cold, and seasick.*

9. Which sentence should begin a new paragraph?
   Ⓐ sentence 14
   Ⓑ sentence 15
   Ⓒ sentence 16
   Ⓓ sentence 17

10. What change should be made in sentence 16?
    Ⓐ Change *November* to *november.*
    Ⓑ Change *ships* to *ships'.*
    Ⓒ Change *ships* to *ship's.*
    Ⓓ Change *spotted* to *spots.*

11. How would sentence 17 look if it were written correctly?
    Ⓐ He cried out, "land ho"!
    Ⓑ "He cried out, land ho!"
    Ⓒ He cried out "land ho!"
    Ⓓ He cried out, "Land ho!"

12. What change should be made in sentence 19?
    Ⓐ Change *Them* to *They.*
    Ⓑ Change *were* to *was.*
    Ⓒ Change the period to a question mark.
    Ⓓ Make no change.

13. What change should be made in sentence 20?
    Ⓐ Change *Mayflower* to *mayflower*.
    Ⓑ Change *anchored* to *will anchor*.
    Ⓒ Change *coast* to *coast'*.
    Ⓓ Change *massachusetts* to *Massachusetts*.

14. What change should be made in sentence 21?
    Ⓐ Change *Pilgrims'* to *Pilgrims*.
    Ⓑ Change *were* to *was*.
    Ⓒ Change *were* to *is*.
    Ⓓ Make no change.

15. How should sentence 22 be written to be a complete sentence?
    Ⓐ They shouted with joy to be leaving the crowded ship.
    Ⓑ Shouting with joy to be leaving the crowded ship.
    Ⓒ To be leaving the crowded ship, shouted with joy.
    Ⓓ Leaving the crowded ship and shouting with joy.

16. What change should be made in sentence 23?
    Ⓐ Change *Pilgrims* to *pilgrims*.
    Ⓑ Change *knowed* to *knew*.
    Ⓒ Change *knowed* to *know*.
    Ⓓ Change *their* to *there*.

17. What is the best way to write sentence 24 as two sentences?
    Ⓐ They searched for a place. To settle they decided on Plymouth.
    Ⓑ They searched. For a place to settle decided on Plymouth.
    Ⓒ They searched for a place to settle. They decided on Plymouth.
    Ⓓ They searched. They decided on Plymouth a place to settle.

18. What change should be made to sentence 25?
    Ⓐ Take out the comma before *but*.
    Ⓑ Change *difficulter* to *most difficult*.
    Ⓒ Change *difficulter* to *more difficulter*.
    Ⓓ Change *difficulter* to *more difficult*.

Read the story in which a polar bear explains how he stays warm.
Then answer questions 19–36.

How I Stay Warm in the Arctic

(1) I live in a frozen world. (2) My home is in the Arctic, an area near the north pole. (3) The word *Arctic* comes from an ancient Greek word that means "country of the great bear." (4) Its so cold in the Arctic that even the ocean freezes in the winter.

(5) Very few animals can live in the icy Far North. (6) The wind and the snow blow fiercely. (7) I stay warm. (8) Let me tell you why. (9) First, I have a nice coat with two layers. (10) The bottom layer are thick and woolly. (11) The hairs of the top layer are very stiff. (12) They is also clear. (13) The suns rays hit the clear hairs. (14) The rays pass threw to my black skin. (15) Dark color hold heat better than light colors.

(16) But there's more to my story about how I stays warm. (17) Beneath my thick fur coat and black skin is a layer of fat called *blubber*. (18) My blubber is like a blanket. (19) It protect me from the freezing temperatures. (20) I have black eyes and a black nose.

(21) I love to swim in the icy Arctic water I can swim for miles without stopping. (22) My waterproof coat and layer of blubber keep me dry and warm. (23) I just shake myself like a dog after a swim.

(24) Sometimes the bitter winds are to fierce for me. (25) Then I dig a cave in a snowbank. (26) Inside, I curl up into a big furry ball and wait for the snowstorm to end. (27) The weather is warmer in the summer than in the winter. (28) During this time, I shed my old fur coat. (29) Then I grow a new one!

19. What change should be made in sentence 2?
   Ⓐ Change *is* to *are*.
   Ⓑ Change *is* to *am*.
   Ⓒ Change *north pole* to *north Pole*.
   Ⓓ Change *north pole* to *North Pole*.

20. What change should be made in sentence 4?
   Ⓐ Change *Its* to *It's*.
   Ⓑ Change *Its* to *Its'*.
   Ⓒ Change *freezes* to *freeze*.
   Ⓓ Make no change.

21. How can sentences 6 and 7 best be combined?
   Ⓐ The wind and the snow blow fiercely and I stay warm.
   Ⓑ The wind and the snow blow fiercely I stay warm.
   Ⓒ The wind and the snow blow fiercely, I stay warm.
   Ⓓ The wind and the snow blow fiercely, but I stay warm.

22. The meaning of sentence 9 would be made clearer by changing *nice* to
   Ⓐ *good*.
   Ⓑ *furry*.
   Ⓒ *bad*.
   Ⓓ *very nice*.

23. What change should be made in sentence 10?
   Ⓐ Change *are* to *will be*.
   Ⓑ Change *are* to *is*.
   Ⓒ Change *are* to *am*.
   Ⓓ Change *are* to *were*.

24. What change should be made in sentence 12?
   Ⓐ Change *They* to *Them*.
   Ⓑ Change *is* to *are*.
   Ⓒ Change *is* to *was*.
   Ⓓ Make no change.

25. What change should be made in sentence 13?
   Ⓐ Change *suns* to *suns'*.
   Ⓑ Change *suns* to *sun's*.
   Ⓒ Change *hit* to *hits*.
   Ⓓ Make no change.

26. What change should be made in sentence 14?
   Ⓐ Change *rays* to *rays'*.
   Ⓑ Change *rays* to *ray's*.
   Ⓒ Change *pass* to *passes*.
   Ⓓ Change *threw* to *through*.

27. What change should be made in sentence 15?
   Ⓐ Change *Dark* to *Darkest*.
   Ⓑ Change *color* to *colors*.
   Ⓒ Change *color* to *color's*.
   Ⓓ Change the period to a question mark.

28. What change should be made in sentence 16?
   Ⓐ Change *to* to *too*.
   Ⓑ Change *stays* to *staying*.
   Ⓒ Change *stays* to *stay*.
   Ⓓ Change *warm* to *warmest*.

29. What change should be made in sentence 19?
   Ⓐ Change *It* to *They*.
   Ⓑ Change *protect* to *protects*.
   Ⓒ Change *protect* to *protected*.
   Ⓓ Change *me* to *I*.

30. Which detail sentence does not belong in the third paragraph?
   Ⓐ sentence 17
   Ⓑ sentence 18
   Ⓒ sentence 19
   Ⓓ sentence 20

31. How would sentence 21 look if it were written correctly?
   Ⓐ I love to swim in the icy Arctic water, I can swim
      for miles without stopping.
   Ⓑ I love to swim in the icy Arctic water but I can swim
      for miles without stopping.
   Ⓒ I love to swim in the icy Arctic water. I can swim
      for miles without stopping.
   Ⓓ I love to swim. In the icy Arctic water. I can swim
      for miles without stopping.

32. What change should be made in sentence 22?
   Ⓐ Change *me* to *I*.
   Ⓑ Change *me* to *us*.
   Ⓒ Add a comma after *dry*.
   Ⓓ Make no change.

33. How can sentence 23 be changed so that it doesn't begin with *I*?
   Ⓐ After a swim, just shake myself like a dog.
   Ⓑ Always shake like a dog after a swim.
   Ⓒ After a swim, I just shake myself like a dog.
   Ⓓ As I shake myself off, I look like a dog.

34. What change should be made in sentence 24?
   Ⓐ Change *are* to *is*.
   Ⓑ Change *to* to *too*.
   Ⓒ Change *to* to *two*.
   Ⓓ Change *me* to *I*.

35. In sentence 26, a more exact word for *big* would be
   Ⓐ *nice*.
   Ⓑ *giant*.
   Ⓒ *biggest*.
   Ⓓ *bigger*.

36. Which sentence should begin a new paragraph?
   Ⓐ sentence 25
   Ⓑ sentence 26
   Ⓒ sentence 27
   Ⓓ sentence 28

Read the story about a man who invented something that is useful to all of us. Then answer questions 37–54.

Bell's Talking Machine

(1) Alexander graham Bell was born in Scotland on March 3, 1847. (2) As a young boy, Bell was full of questions. (3) One time he put his ear to the ground in a wheat field. (4) He asked himself, "Can you hear wheat grow"?

(5) When Bell growed up, he became a teacher. (6) He taught at the Boston School For The Deaf. (7) Bell was interested in human speech. (8) He knew that sound travel through the air. (9) He knew that a telegraph could send signals electrically by wire. (10) He had an idea. (11) He would try to send speech sounds by wire too. (12) First, he would turn the sounds into an electric current. (13) He would send the current over a wire. (14) A machine would receive the current and then turn back into speech. (15) In 1874, Bell hired a helper named Thomas Watson. (16) Together, the men worked on Bell's idea for a talking machine.

(17) On March 10, 1876, Bell and Watson were working on separate floors in they're shop. (18) Bell suddenly called out, "Mr. Watson come here!" (19) Watson came up the stairs. (20) He had heard every word Bell had spoken—over the talking machine!

(21) Several months later, Bell will introduce his telephone at a fair in Philadelphia. (22) He won first prize for his invention. (23) But the telephone wasnt an instant success. (24) Many people laughed at Bells machine. (25) Within a few years, though, thousands of familys in the United States had a telephone in their home. (26) Today many people have cell phones.

(27) Alexander Graham Bell died on August 29, 1922, at the age of 75. (28) On that day, all telephone service stopped for one minute to honor the great inventor.

37. What change should be made in sentence 1?
    Ⓐ Change *Alexander graham Bell* to *Alexander Graham Bell.*
    Ⓑ Change *Alexander graham Bell* to *Alexander graham bell.*
    Ⓒ Change *Scotland* to *scotland.*
    Ⓓ Change the period to an exclamation point.

38. How would sentence 4 look if it were written correctly?
    Ⓐ He asked himself, "can you hear wheat grow"?
    Ⓑ He asked himself "Can you hear wheat grow"?
    Ⓒ He asked himself, "Can you hear wheat grow?"
    Ⓓ He asked himself, "Can you hear wheat grow."

39. What change should be made in sentence 5?
    Ⓐ Change *growed* to *grew.*
    Ⓑ Change *growed* to *will grow.*
    Ⓒ Change *he* to *him.*
    Ⓓ Make no change.

40. In sentence 6, *Boston School For The Deaf* should be changed to
    Ⓐ *boston school for the deaf.*
    Ⓑ *Boston School for the deaf.*
    Ⓒ *Boston school for the deaf.*
    Ⓓ *Boston School for the Deaf.*

41. What change should be made in sentence 8?
    Ⓐ Change *knew* to *new.*
    Ⓑ Change *knew* to *knowed.*
    Ⓒ Change *travel* to *travels.*
    Ⓓ Change *through* to *threw.*

42. How can sentence 10 be changed so that it doesn't begin with *he*?
    Ⓐ Him got an idea.
    Ⓑ An idea came to him.
    Ⓒ An idea had he.
    Ⓓ Had an idea.

43. The meaning of sentence 13 would be made clearer by
    Ⓐ ending the sentence with an exclamation point.
    Ⓑ adding the adjective *electric* before *wire*.
    Ⓒ removing the pronoun *He*.
    Ⓓ beginning the sentence with the adverb *Then*.

44. What is the best way to improve sentence 14?
    Ⓐ A machine would receive the current. Then turn back into speech.
    Ⓑ A machine would receive the current, and then turn back into speech.
    Ⓒ A machine would receive the current and then turn it back into speech.
    Ⓓ A machine would receive and turn back the current.

45. Which sentence should begin a new paragraph?
    Ⓐ sentence 13
    Ⓑ sentence 14
    Ⓒ sentence 15
    Ⓓ sentence 16

46. What change should be made in sentence 17?
    Ⓐ Change *they're* to *their*.
    Ⓑ Change *they're* to *there*.
    Ⓒ Change *March* to *march*.
    Ⓓ Make no change.

47. How would sentence 18 look if it were written correctly?
    Ⓐ Bell suddenly called out "Mr. Watson come here!"
    Ⓑ Bell suddenly called out, "Mr. Watson come here"!
    Ⓒ Bell suddenly called out, "Mr. Watson, come here!"
    Ⓓ Bell suddenly called out, "Mr. Watson." "Come here!"

48. The meaning of sentence 19 would be made clearer by changing *came* to
    Ⓐ *went.*
    Ⓑ *raced.*
    Ⓒ *come.*
    Ⓓ *coming.*

49. What change should be made in sentence 21?
Ⓐ Change *months* to *month*.
Ⓑ Change *will introduce* to *introduces*.
Ⓒ Change *will introduce* to *introduced*.
Ⓓ Change *fair* to *Fair*.

50. What change should be made in sentence 23?
Ⓐ Change *wasnt* to *wasnt'*.
Ⓑ Change *wasnt* to *wasn't*.
Ⓒ Change *wasnt* to *weren't*.
Ⓓ Make no change.

51. What change should be made in sentence 24?
Ⓐ Change *laughed* to *laught*.
Ⓑ Change *laughed* to *laughs*.
Ⓒ Change *Bells* to *Bells'*.
Ⓓ Change *Bells* to *Bell's*.

52. What change should be made in sentence 25?
Ⓐ Change *familys* to *familys'*.
Ⓑ Change *familys* to *families*.
Ⓒ Change *their* to *there*.
Ⓓ Change *their* to *they're*.

53. Which detail sentence does not belong in the fourth paragraph?
Ⓐ sentence 23
Ⓑ sentence 24
Ⓒ sentence 25
Ⓓ sentence 26

54. The meaning of sentence 28 would be made clearer by changing *great* to
Ⓐ *big*.
Ⓑ *nice*.
Ⓒ *talented*.
Ⓓ *very great*.

PART II — In Lessons 31–37 you write. Use what you've learned in Part I to *WRITE!*

LESSON 31

DESCRIPTIONS

To describe is to tell about people, places, or things. When you describe something in writing, you should use strong, colorful words and details. They will create images, or pictures, in readers' minds. These are called descriptions.

Here is a sample writing prompt for a description.

> *Write a description of a fun place to be.*

Read the description. It was written in response to the prompt. Then read the Writing Tips to learn more about descriptions.

Writing Tips

✳ Show instead of tell. Choose words that make your subject seem to come alive for readers.

✳ Before writing, use your five senses to come up with words that describe the subject. When describing a place, for example, ask yourself some questions.

✳ What can I see there?

✳ What can I hear there?

✳ Can I smell, touch, or taste anything there?

✳ Choose sense details and strong, colorful words to build the description.

✳ Create a clear beginning, middle, and ending. Put the details in an order that makes sense.

✳ If possible, use comparisons to paint pictures with words. If there are pine needles on the ground, do they "rest like a soft, brown blanket"?

It's Sunday afternoon. My cousins, aunts, and uncles gather in Grandma's backyard for a picnic. We all breathe in the smells of Grandma's cooking. Barbecue smoke rises in the air. The adults tease each other about who is the best cook. The rest of us play hide-and-seek in the bushes. The winners' cheers fill the air. Grandma shakes out a smooth tablecloth. It looks like a big sail on the picnic table. She sets out pitchers of cold milk. Then she puts out glasses and big red plates. The plates look like big polka dots on the white tablecloth. Grandma announces that dinner is ready, and we all run to the table.

USING GRAPHIC ORGANIZERS

Before you write, use graphic organizers, or information pictures. They can help you think about, gather, and sort information for your description.

The person who wrote the description of the picnic on page 76 might have used a Senses Chart, such as the one below.

Sight	cousins, aunts, uncles, Grandma, bushes, tablecloth, table, pitchers, glasses, plates
Sound	talking, cheers
Taste	cold milk
Touch	smooth tablecloth
Smell	Grandma's cooking, barbecue smoke

Writers can use a Senses Chart to gather information about some or all of the five senses. This information can be used in descriptions.

The writer might also have used a Describing-Words Web to gather colorful words for the description on page 76. How might the writer have filled in this web? One describing word is already given. Fill in the other ovals with words that describe the picnic.

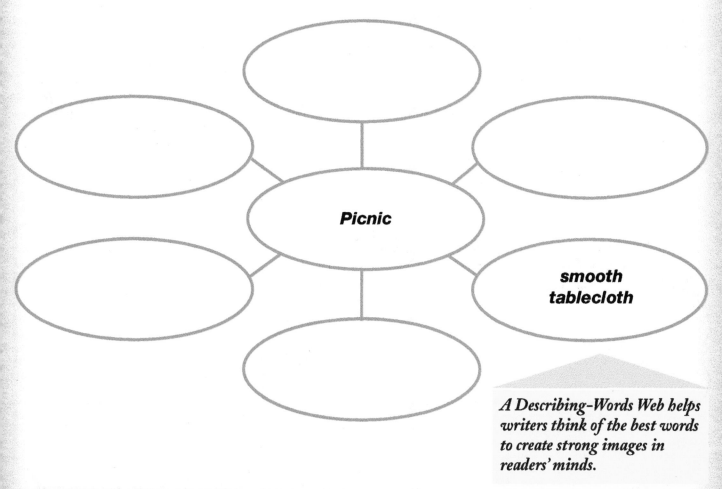

Picnic

smooth tablecloth

A Describing-Words Web helps writers think of the best words to create strong images in readers' minds.

Score: 4

Read the description below. It was written in response to the prompt on page 76. This description scored a 4 on a scale that ranges from 1 to 4 (with 4 being the best). Next, read the comments and think about why this description scored a 4.

1

One of my favorite places is the skating rink. First, you enter a heated room that has sturdy wooden benches. This is where you change into your skates. Then you go into the rink. Its as cold as a refrigerator. The ice looks like smooth glass. Lots of people are skating. The beginners creep along. Some hold the rail. Other skaters swoosh by. They are very graceful. Were they born on skates. The loudspeaker plays rock music. You skate and skate. The warm and salty smell of popcorn finally leads you to the snack bar. You leave the rink tired and happy. You look forward to your next visit.

Your Turn

Now it's your turn to help the writer. Find and fix the errors in the description. Go back to the pages in green if you need help.

1. Find and fix the incorrect **contraction**. See pp. 52–53.
2. Find and fix the error in **end punctuation**. See pp. 38–39.

2

PARTNER COMMENTS

Right away you said that the place is a skating rink. I could see it. I felt as if I were at the rink with you. This is a good description!

3

TEACHER COMMENTS

4

▲ Thank you for telling me in the first sentence what you're describing.
▲ I can easily imagine the rink because of your details.
▲ I like the comparisons about the rink and the ice.
▲ Colorful words like sturdy, creep, and swoosh make your description come alive.
▲ You vary your sentences, and you present your details in an order that makes sense. Good!

Score:

Read the description and the comments that follow. Think about why this description scored a 3.

1

I like the skating rink. First, I put on my skates in a warm room. Its cold inside the rink. The ice is very smooth and I see lots of skaters and I also see beginners who creep along and hold the rail. Other skaters are really graceful. They look as if they skate all the time. I here rock music in the background. The warm smell of popcorn leads me to the snack bar. I look forward to my next visit

Your Turn

Now it's your turn to help the writer. Find and fix the errors in the description. Go back to the pages in green if you need help.

1. Indent the **paragraph**. See pp. 56–57.
2. Find and fix the **contraction** error. See pp. 52–53.
3. Find the **run-on sentence**. Rewrite it as shorter sentences. See pp. 44–45.
4. Find and fix the incorrect **homophone**. See pp. 36–37.
5. Find and fix the sentence that has no **end punctuation**. See pp. 38–39.

2

PARTNER COMMENTS

I liked reading about the rink. You gave some details, but I would have liked more. You wrote the description in an order that makes sense. I could follow it easily.

3

TEACHER COMMENTS

4

▲ Thank you for introducing the subject in your opening sentence.
▲ Your ideas flow in a way that makes sense.
▲ You need more sense words.
▲ Use some variety with your **sentences.** See pp. 38–39 and 60–61 for help.

Score:

2

Read the description and the comments that follow.
Think about why this description scored a 2.

1

I like skating. I go to the rink. I sit on the benchs. I put on my skates. It is cold and smooth. I see lots of skaters. There are beginners who arent fast. The good skaters is the fast ones. I here music. Skate a lot. The popcorn smells good to me Then I leave the rink. I am tired. I no I will visit again

2

PARTNER COMMENTS

I could tell that you were describing a skating rink. You made a lot of mistakes, though. Your sentences are short. Your description was hard to understand.

Your Turn

Now it's your turn to help the writer. Find and fix the errors in the description. Go back to the pages in green if you need help.

1. Indent the **paragraph**. See pp. 56–57.
2. Find and fix the incorrect **plural noun**. See pp. 6–7.
3. Find and fix the **contraction** error. See pp. 52–53.
4. Find and fix the error in **subject-verb agreement**. See pp. 24–25.
5. Find and fix the two incorrect **homophones**. See pp. 36–37.
6. Find the **sentence fragment**. Rewrite it as a complete sentence. See pp. 40–41.
7. Find and fix the two sentences that have no **end punctuation**. See pp. 38–39.

TEACHER COMMENTS

3

4

▲ I know that you are talking about a skating rink, but you need more details.
▲ Your paragraph is so choppy that I can't see the skating rink in my mind.
▲ You need to add more **exact words** to your description. See pp. 26–27 and 32–33 for help.
▲ Change some **types** of **sentences**, and **join** some **sentences** to make longer ones. See pp. 38–39, 42–43, and 60–61.

Score:

Read the description and the comments that follow. Think about why this description scored a 1.

I put on my skates and lookd all around. The ice cold and smooth. The skaters and me goes around and around. Once I went to canada. Their is music here. this place has good popcorn smells It is lots of fun

2

PARTNER COMMENTS

I wasn't sure what you were describing. You should have started by naming the place. Why did you mention Canada? Is the rink there? This is not really a description even though you used words like *cold* and *smooth*.

3

TEACHER COMMENTS

▲ I can't tell what place you are describing. It's clear that you like the place, but I need more details to know why.

▲ Your ideas aren't in an order that makes sense.

▲ You shouldn't mention Canada in this paragraph unless it has something to do with the place you're describing.

▲ You need to vary your **words** and types of **sentences.** See pp. 26–27, 32–33, 38–39, and 60–61 for help.

Your Turn

Now it's your turn to help the writer. Find and fix the errors in the description. Go back to the pages in green if you need help.

1. Indent the **paragraph**. See pp. 56–57.

2. Find and fix the incorrect **past-time verb**. See pp. 16–17.

3. Find and fix the **sentence fragment**. See pp. 40–41.

4. Find and fix the incorrect **pronoun**. See pp. 12–13.

5. Find and fix the error in **subject-verb agreement**. See pp. 22–23.

6. Find and fix the two **capitalization** errors. See pp. 46–49.

7. Find and fix the incorrect **homophone**. See pp. 36–37.

8. Find and fix the two sentences that are missing **end punctuation**. See pp. 38–39.

4

USING A RUBRIC TO SCORE DESCRIPTIONS

This rubric is based on a point scale of 1 to 4. It was used to score the descriptions on pages 78–81. Use this rubric to remember what is important in descriptions.

4 A score of 4 means that the writer

- ❑ connects the writing directly to the prompt.
- ❑ almost always uses the correct forms of words.
- ❑ almost always uses capitalization, punctuation, and indentation correctly.
- ❑ almost always uses clear and complete sentences and includes variety in sentences.
- ❑ introduces the subject clearly at the beginning of the description.
- ❑ creates a clear beginning, middle, and ending.
- ❑ uses many interesting details and colorful, sense words to create a strong image for readers.
- ❑ uses comparisons that make the image clear.

2 A score of 2 means that the writer

- ❑ connects the writing to the prompt in a general way.
- ❑ uses some incorrect forms of words and some incorrect capitalization, punctuation, or indentation.
- ❑ includes little variety in sentences and uses some run-on sentences or sentence fragments.
- ❑ presents the subject somewhere within the description.
- ❑ creates a weak beginning, middle, or ending.
- ❑ uses too few interesting details or colorful words to create a strong image for readers.
- ❑ uses no comparisons or uses them unsuccessfully.

3 A score of 3 means that the writer

- ❑ connects the writing to the prompt.
- ❑ usually uses the correct forms of words.
- ❑ usually uses capitalization, punctuation, and indentation correctly.
- ❑ usually uses clear and complete sentences and includes some variety in sentences.
- ❑ introduces the subject toward the beginning of the description.
- ❑ creates a beginning, middle, and ending.
- ❑ uses some interesting details and colorful, sense words to create a clear image for readers.
- ❑ uses some simple comparisons.

1 A score of 1 means that the writer

- ❑ does not successfully connect the writing to the prompt.
- ❑ uses many incorrect forms of words and often uses incorrect capitalization, punctuation, or indentation.
- ❑ includes almost no variety in sentences and uses several run-on sentences or sentence fragments.
- ❑ creates an unclear beginning, middle, or ending.
- ❑ names the subject in an unclear way or not at all.
- ❑ uses words and details that fail to create a clear image for readers.
- ❑ uses no comparisons.

SCORING DESCRIPTIONS

Now it's your turn to score some descriptions. The four descriptions on pages 83 and 84 were written in response to this prompt.

> *Write a description of a place that you like to visit.*

Read each description. Write a few comments about it. Then give it a score from 1 to 4. Think about what you've learned in this lesson as you match each description with its correct score.

Model A

Score:

I no an island in Maine and there are roses that smell good there. There are berrys that smell good to. There is swimming. Its cold. The waves washes over you. You can float on your back. Never want to leave. That's for sure

Comments: _____
_____
_____
_____
_____
_____
_____
_____
_____

Model B

Score:

An island in Maine is a great place to visit. There are roses and green bushes and the roses smell sweet. There is a place to swim. The water is really cold. Sometimes water washes over you. Other times its better to float. This island is a place you will never want to leave

Comments: _____
_____
_____
_____
_____
_____
_____
_____

Model C

Score:

Bushs with flowers is all around. Me and my dog goes to a swimming place. The water was cold It was like ice cubes. It is by the water. the waves flied over my face. I will go back. For sure. It is my favorite place

Comments: _____
_____
_____
_____
_____
_____
_____
_____

Model D

Score:

There is a rocky island in Maine that is a great place to visit. Green bushes and red roses grow along the shore. The roses smell sweet. There is a great place for swimming. Do you know how it feels to get out of bed on a winter morning? Getting dunked in that water feels the same way. Its cold! Sometimes waves splash over your face. Sometimes it's calm, and you can float on you're back and stare at the sky. This island is a place you'll never want to leave.

Comments: _____
_____
_____
_____
_____
_____
_____
_____

WRITING A DESCRIPTION

Now you get to write your own description.
Use the prompt below.

> *Write a description of your own favorite place.*

When You Write Your Description

1. **Think about** what you want to write. Close your eyes and picture the place you want to describe. Ask yourself some questions.
   - What do I see there?
   - What do I hear?
   - What can I touch and what does it feel like?
   - Can I smell or taste anything there?

   Use graphic organizers to gather and sort your information.

2. **Write** your first draft. Name the place you are describing at the beginning of the paragraph. Then describe the place with colorful words that make the place seem real. Use comparisons if they help your description.

3. **Read** your draft. Use the checklist that your teacher will give you to review your writing.

4. **Edit** your description until it paints a clear picture of the place you're describing.

5. **Proofread** your description one last time.

6. **Write** a neat copy of your description and give it to your partner.

Work with a Partner

7. **Read** your partner's description.

8. **Score** your partner's description from 1 to 4, using the rubric on page 82. Then complete the Partner Comments sheet that your teacher will give you. Tell what you liked about the description and what you think would make it better.

9. **Switch** papers.

10. **Think about** your partner's comments. Read your description again. Make any changes that you think will improve your description.

11. **Write** a neat final copy of your description.

Making Connections

- As you read books and magazines and watch TV, notice how people use details related to the five senses. These details create powerful images.

- Jot notes in your journal about people, places, or things that would be fun to describe. Remember that when you describe people, you can add details about how they behave. Does someone laugh, sing, or frown a lot? Save your notes. They can be ideas for future writing.

- Practice using sense words with a friend. Think of an object that your friend knows about, but don't say what it is. Use several sense words to describe the object. Can your friend guess what you are describing? Take turns doing this.

PERSONAL NARRATIVES

You write stories about all kinds of things. Sometimes you even write about your own life.

A narrative is a true or made-up story. A personal narrative is a true story. It tells about things that have happened in your own life.

Here is a sample writing prompt for a personal narrative.

> *Write about a time when you made a new friend.*

Read the personal narrative. It was written in response to the prompt. Then read the Writing Tips to learn more about personal narratives.

Writing Tips

* Remember that when you write a personal narrative, you are telling a true story, a story about you!

* You can write about anything in your life: big or small, happy or sad. Things happen to you every day, and you can write about any of them.

* Write from your own point of view. Use words such as *I, me,* and *my* in your story.

* Think of a good title for your story.

* Make your story come alive. Write as if you were telling the story to a friend.

* When you speak, you stop and start. You may make your voice louder or softer to make a point. Capitalization and punctuation can give this kind of "voice" to your writing.

* Present your story events in an order that makes sense. Create a clear beginning, middle, and ending.

Making a New Friend

My dog Ginger and I arrived at the beach, and I slipped Ginger's harness off. She raced across the sand and jumped straight into the lake with a huge splash. She looked back happily in my direction.

I tossed a toy for Ginger to fetch, but another dog got to it first. The new dog brought the toy to me. I threw the toy again, and both dogs swam for it. The three of us played toss and fetch for a long time.

Then I heard a woman call her dog, Lucky. Our new friend Lucky did not know whether to stay or go. Ginger barked because she wanted to play more with Lucky. But Lucky had to go. I know that Ginger and I will soon see Lucky again at the beach.

USING GRAPHIC ORGANIZERS

Before you write, use graphic organizers, or information pictures. They can help you think about, gather, and sort ideas for your personal narrative.

The person who wrote the story on page 86 might have used a Character Web, such as the one below.

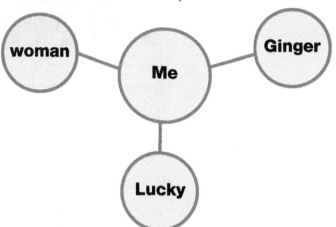

A Character Web helps writers organize details about the characters in a story. In a personal narrative, the writer is always the main character.

An Events Chart can also help writers plan a personal narrative. How might the writer of the story on page 86 have used this chart? Fill in the boxes.

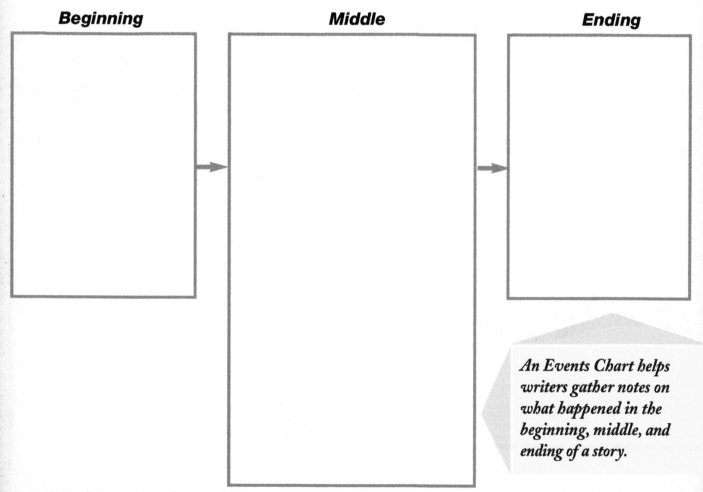

Beginning

Middle

Ending

An Events Chart helps writers gather notes on what happened in the beginning, middle, and ending of a story.

Score: **4**

Read the personal narrative below. It was written in response to the prompt on page 86. Next, read the comments and think about why this story scored a 4.

Making a New Friend

I remember the summer when my Gram and I found Sal. We were picking ripe berries behind Grams house. We saw a kitten under a bush. It looked skinny and scared. It probably didn't have a home. We wondered what to do with it.

Gram could take the kitten home, but she had a dog, Hal. Hal might not want a kitten. We didn't know if the kitten was a girl, but we named it Sal. That sounded like Hal's name. We hoped that would help.

Gram, Sal, and me headed for the house. We went in, and Hal seemed interested. He didn't bark. We let him sniff the kitten. Hal liked Sal! We all had a new friend.

Your Turn

Now it's your turn to help the writer. Find and fix the errors in the personal narrative. Go back to the pages in green if you need help.

1. Find and fix the incorrect **possessive noun.** See pp. 8–9.
2. Find and fix the incorrect **pronoun.** See pp. 12–13.

TEACHER COMMENTS 4

▲ Your title lets me know what to expect.
▲ The story flows well, with all events connected. I feel as if I'm "there" with you.
▲ I like the way you share what you and Gram are thinking.
▲ Your details make Hal come alive.
▲ You use paragraphs correctly.
▲ You make good word choices, and you use variety in your sentences.

PARTNER COMMENTS

Your story grabbed my interest from the start. You and all the other characters came alive. The events moved along, and the ending was very good.

2

3

Read the personal narrative and the comments that follow.
Think about why this story scored a 3.

1

Gram's Friend

Gram and I were picking berrys. We found a kitten behind the house. The kitten was under a bush. The kitten was scared. It probably didnt have a home. We wondered what to do with it.

Gram could take the kitten home. But Gram had Hal, a dog. Would Hal want a kitten? We called the kitten Sal. It was like Hals name. We hoped Hal would like that.

Gram Sal and me headed for the door. We went in, and Hal seemed surprised. He didn't bark, but he sniffed around. Hal liked Sal. Gram and me also liked Sal. We all had a new friend.

2

Your Turn

Now it's your turn to help the writer. Find and fix the errors in the personal narrative. Go back to the pages in green if you need help.

1. Find and fix the incorrect **plural noun.** See pp. 6–7.
2. Find and fix the **contraction** error. See pp. 52–53.
3. Find and fix the incorrect **possessive noun.** See pp. 8–9.
4. Find and fix the error with **commas in a series.** See pp. 50–51.
5. Find and fix the two incorrect **pronouns.** See pp. 12–13.

PARTNER COMMENTS

The opening of your story wasn't strong. The events didn't go together. I read the story anyway to find out what happened to the kitten. The story never totally grabbed my interest, though.

3

TEACHER COMMENTS

4

▲ Your ideas are nicely connected.
▲ Is Gram the only one who made a friend? What is a better title?
▲ Nice job describing Hal! I'd like to know a little more about Gram also.
▲ Make sure you vary the kinds of **sentences** you use. See pp. 38–39 and 60–61 for help.

Score:

Read the personal narrative and the comments that follow.
Think about why this story scored a 2.

1

Gram

A kitten was behind the house. Gram and me seen it. The kitten was small. It did not have a Home.

Gram had a dog at home. The dog was Hal. Hal was brown. Gram brought the kitten home with her would a dog like a kitten?

We called the kitten Sal We went to the house. Hal was inside. Her and I went in. Hal was there. He sniffed and smelld around. Hal did not bark at all. I was glad four that

Your Turn

Now it's your turn to help the writer. Find and fix the errors in the personal narrative. Go back to the pages in green if you need help.

1. Find and fix the **paragraph** that isn't indented. See pp. 56–57.
2. Find and fix the two **pronoun** errors. See pp. 12–13.
3. Find and fix the two incorrect **verbs** that show past time. See pp. 16–19.
4. Find and fix the **capitalization** error. See pp. 46–47.
5. Find and fix the **run-on sentence.** See pp. 44–45.
6. Find and fix the two errors in **end punctuation.** See pp. 38–39.
7. Find and fix the incorrect **homophone.** See pp. 36–37.

2

PARTNER COMMENTS

Your title didn't tell what the story was about. Some of the details didn't seem to belong in the story, and I think some details are missing. It was hard for me to follow the events. Also, the other characters didn't seem real. Your ending left me hanging.

3

TEACHER COMMENTS

4

▲ Is this story only about Gram? Write a title that tells more about the story.
▲ I'd like more **details.** See pp. 58–59 for help.
▲ Use more **exact** words. See pp. 26–27 and 32–33.
▲ Use more variety in your **sentences.** See pp. 38–39 and 60–61.
▲ **Join** some short **sentences** to make longer ones. See pp. 42–43.

Read the personal narrative and the comments that follow.
Think about why this story scored a 1.

A lady seen a kitten. Behind her house. The kitten was under a tree. the kitten was small. The kitten didnt have a home. The lady had a dog the dog was Hal. The lady knowed things about dogs and kittens. The lady took the kitten home. Hal was their. He was inside the house. The lady took sal in the house. Hal did not bark. Hal sat down. Would Hal be a good friend? They was at the ladys house.

PARTNER COMMENTS

2

You didn't follow the prompt. The story wasn't even about your life. It was about a lady, and you didn't seem to know her. The story didn't grab my attention because there weren't enough details. It was hard to picture the characters. Also, where is your title?

TEACHER COMMENTS

3

▲ The story should have a title and be about your life.
▲ Use more **pronouns** in place of nouns.
   See pp. 10–11 for help.
▲ Use more **interesting, colorful words.**
   See pp. 26–27 and 32–33.
▲ Sometimes **join short sentences** to make longer sentences. See pp. 38–39 and 40–41.
▲ Use more variety with **sentences.** See pp. 60–61.

Your Turn

Now it's your turn to help the writer. Find and fix the errors in the personal narrative. Go back to the pages in green if you need help.

1. Indent the **paragraph.** See pp. 56–57.

2. Find and fix the two incorrect **verbs** that show past time. See pp. 18–19.

3. Find and fix the **sentence fragment.** See pp. 40–41.

4. Find and fix the two errors in **capitalization.** See pp. 46–49.

5. Find and fix the **contraction** error. See pp. 52–53.

6. Find and fix the **run-on sentence.** See pp. 44–45.

7. Find and fix the incorrect **homophone.** See pp. 36–37.

8. Find and fix the error in **subject-verb agreement.** See pp. 24–25.

9. Find and fix the incorrect **possessive noun.** See pp. 8–9.

4

USING A RUBRIC TO SCORE PERSONAL NARRATIVES

This rubric is based on a point scale of 1 to 4. It was used to score the personal narratives on pages 88–91. Use this rubric to remember what is important in personal narratives.

4 A score of 4 means that the writer

- ❑ connects the writing directly to the prompt.
- ❑ almost always uses the correct forms of words.
- ❑ almost always uses capitalization and punctuation correctly.
- ❑ almost always uses clear and complete sentences and includes variety in sentences.
- ❑ uses interesting words.
- ❑ creates an attention-getting title that relates to the story.
- ❑ creates a clear beginning, middle, and ending.
- ❑ tells the story from his or her point of view and seems connected to the story.
- ❑ presents many interesting story details, including thoughts and feelings.
- ❑ begins a new paragraph for each change of idea.

2 A score of 2 means that the writer

- ❑ connects the writing to the prompt in a general way.
- ❑ uses some incorrect forms of words and some incorrect capitalization or punctuation.
- ❑ includes little variety in sentences and uses some run-on sentences or sentence fragments.
- ❑ uses mostly simple words.
- ❑ creates a title that relates somewhat to the story.
- ❑ creates a weak beginning, middle, or ending.
- ❑ usually tells the story from his or her point of view but may not seem connected to the story.
- ❑ presents weak story details.
- ❑ makes some paragraphing errors.

3 A score of 3 means that the writer

- ❑ connects the writing to the prompt.
- ❑ usually uses the correct forms of words.
- ❑ usually uses capitalization and punctuation correctly.
- ❑ usually uses clear and complete sentences and includes some variety in sentences.
- ❑ uses some interesting words.
- ❑ creates a title that generally relates to the story.
- ❑ tells the story from his or her point of view.
- ❑ creates a beginning, middle, or ending.
- ❑ presents some interesting story details, including some thoughts and feelings.
- ❑ usually begins a new paragraph for each change of idea.

1 A score of 1 means that the writer

- ❑ does not successfully connect the writing to the prompt.
- ❑ uses many incorrect forms of words and often uses incorrect capitalization or punctuation.
- ❑ includes almost no variety in sentences and uses many run-on sentences or sentence fragments.
- ❑ uses simple words.
- ❑ creates a poor title or no title at all.
- ❑ creates an unclear beginning, middle, or ending.
- ❑ usually doesn't tell the story from his or her point of view.
- ❑ presents story details that are often unclear.
- ❑ makes many paragraphing errors.

SCORING PERSONAL NARRATIVES

Now it's your turn to score some personal narratives. The four stories on pages 93 and 94 were written in response to this prompt.

> *Write about a time when you faced a fear.*

Read each personal narrative. Write a few comments about it. Then give it a score from 1 to 4. Think about what you've learned in this lesson as you match each story with its correct score.

Model A

Score: ▽

The Big Ocean

I was afraid of that water. Ten of us were waiting to take our swimming test. I lived by the ocean. but I didn't usually swim here. Maybe that's why I was scared.

It was my turn, but I didn't want to jump in. My feet felt stuck. I felt chicken, and I couldn't move. Some had jumped in, but were they safe?

Then I saw some of my buddys. They were fine. I jumped in. The water was dark cold and choppy. I had to swim. I headed for the shore. Me and my friends passed the test.

Comments: _____
_____
_____
_____
_____
_____
_____
_____

Model B

Score: ▽

My Brother had a test. It was swimming. At the water. My brother liked the water. This water was dark and cold. He didnt want to jump in. Why jump in for just a test. It was not safe. He new it was not safe. It was dark and choppy and cold. It was his turn. His feet were stuck still. He wanted to be safe. some jumped in but were they safe. He heared them cry out. They was safe. He jumped in. Then the cold and dark water and looking at the shore. he made it.

Comments: _____
_____
_____
_____
_____
_____
_____

Model C

Score:

The Big Jump

I never knew water could look so scary. My buddies and me were waiting to take our swimming test. I had never been afraid of the water. I had never been swimming here, though. Maybe that's why I was so scared.

It was my turn, but it was like my bare feet were glued to the float. I felt chicken, but at least I was safe. Others were already in the water, but I couldnt see them. Were they safe? Then I saw some of my buddies. They were fine. I snapped to and dived in. I knew what I had to do. I swam the distance to shore. I faced my fear and passed the test.

Comments: _____
_____
_____
_____
_____
_____
_____
_____

Model D

Score:

Jumping

I had to pass a swimming test. So did my friends. Me and them was at the water. I looked at it. It was dark and I was scared and I wanted to leave and be safe.

I wasnt scared of the water before. my family lived by the water. But this place was different. I had never been here before. It was new. I did not like it. I did not want to jump into that water. It was my turn to jump in. I felt stuck. My feet would not move. some others did jump in. I couldnt see them. Were they safe. Then I heared them. They were safe. I new it was safe. I jumped in I made it to land. I passed the test.

Comments: _____
_____
_____
_____
_____
_____
_____
_____

WRITING A PERSONAL NARRATIVE

Now you get to write your own personal narrative. Use the prompt below.

> *Write about a time in your life when you did a favor for a friend.*

When You Write Your Personal Narrative

1. **Think about** what you want to write. Ask yourself some questions.
   - Where and when does the story take place?
   - Who else besides me is in the story?
   - What are the important events?
   - How does the story end?

   Use graphic organizers to gather and sort your information.

2. **Write** your first draft. Let your ideas flow. Always remember, though, that the personal narrative you are telling is true and about you.

3. **Read** your draft. Use the checklist that your teacher will give you to review your writing.

4. **Edit** your story. Make changes until your story flows.

5. **Proofread** your story one last time.

6. **Write** a neat copy of your story and give it to your partner.

Work with a Partner

7. **Read** your partner's personal narrative.

8. **Score** your partner's story from 1 to 4, using the rubric on page 92. Then complete the Partner Comments sheet that your teacher will give you. Tell what you liked about the story and what you think would make it better.

9. **Switch** papers.

10. **Think about** your partner's comments. Read your story again. Make any changes that you think will improve your personal narrative.

11. **Write** a neat final copy of your personal narrative.

Making Connections

- When you read about famous people, think about the many little stories that make up each person's life. Many things happened in Abraham Lincoln's life, for example. He could have written a story about learning to read. He could have written another story about becoming president and yet another story about the Civil War.

- In your journal, write notes about things that happened to you this week. Did you make a friend? Learn something new? Score a point? Feel deep sadness? Have a bright idea? Your notes could be ideas for future stories.

- Make a timeline of your life each year. Then you can use the events on the timeline in future personal narratives.

FICTIONAL NARRATIVES

Sometimes you write stories that are true. And sometimes you write stories that you make up. A **fictional narrative** is a story that you make up.

Here is a sample writing prompt for a fictional narrative.

> *Write a story about someone who finds something.*

Read the fictional narrative. It was written in response to the prompt. Then read the Writing Tips to learn more about fictional narratives.

Writing Tips

❖ Your story should have three main parts.

Beginning

- **Setting** This tells where and when the story takes place.
- **Characters** These are the people or animals in the story. Create one main character. You may also create other characters, who work with or against the main character. Your characters will come alive if you have them talk to each other.
- **Problem** This is something the characters have to deal with.

Middle

- **Plot** This is the action of the story. The plot is made up of the events that tell how the characters deal with the problem.

Ending

- **Solution** This tells how the problem turns out.

❖ Create a title that relates to the story.

A Box of Memories

"Look in this box!" called Eddie. He and his friend Jay were cleaning the basement one summer day. They were throwing out empty boxes, but one box was not empty. "It's a good thing I looked inside," said Eddie, "because these are my old baby things." Jay made a face, but Eddie paid no attention.

Eddie reached into the box and pulled out books that he used to read. He found a wind-up mouse that would scurry across the floor. He lifted out his old blanket. "It still feels the same," Eddie said.

Jay thought that it looked like an old, dirty blanket.

"It's soft and warm," said Eddie.

Eddie wondered what to do with his old things. Jay said to toss them, but Eddie decided to keep them. He carefully closed the box and sealed it with tape. One day he would open the box and be surprised again.

USING GRAPHIC ORGANIZERS

Before you write, use graphic organizers. They can help you think about, gather, and sort ideas for your fictional narrative.

The person who wrote the fictional narrative on page 96 might have used the following Character and Setting Chart.

Who:	Eddie, Jay
Where:	the basement
When:	one summer day

A Character and Setting Chart helps writers set the stage for a story. The chart tells who is in the story and where and when the story takes place.

The writer of the story also might have used a Beginning, Middle, and Ending Chart to map out the story. If you had been the writer, what would you have written? Fill in the boxes to tell what happened in the beginning, in the middle, and in the ending of the story.

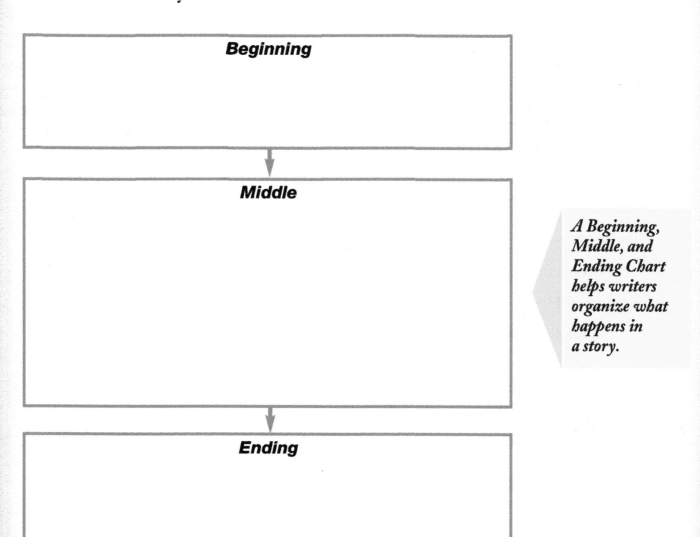

Beginning

Middle

A Beginning, Middle, and Ending Chart helps writers organize what happens in a story.

Ending

Score:

Read the fictional narrative below. It was written in response to the prompt on page 96. Next, read the comments and think about why this story scored a 4.

The Secret Room

"Where did I put that book?" Hannah mumbled. She knew that her friend Maria would love to read the story on this rainy afternoon. Hannah beamed a flashlight into her closet. She saw something surprising. On the back wall was a door that Hannah had never seen before.

Hannah pulled on the knob, but nothing happened. Then Maria joined in. The two pulled really hard. Maybe the door was locked. The girls searched for a key behind clothes and shoes and boxes. Then Hannah felt something cold and heavy on a high shelf. "Maria, I think I found it!

Hannah put the key into the lock. The door opened into a small room that smelled like the past. Spider webs drooped. Dust covered everything. The girls spotted an old trunk in the corner. "Wow! Its better than the book," Hannah exclaimed.

Your Turn

Now it's your turn to help the writer. Find and fix the errors in the fictional narrative. Go back to the pages in green if you need help.

1. Find and fix the missing **quotation mark** before or after a character's words. See pp. 54–55.
2. Find and fix the **contraction** error. See pp. 52–53.

TEACHER COMMENTS

4

▲ Your title gets my attention.
▲ The beginning of the story lets me know that there will be something to solve.
▲ Having Hannah speak to Maria helps make these characters come alive for me.
▲ You present the events in an order that is easy to follow and makes me want to read more.
▲ The details help me picture the secret room.
▲ Your ending tells me that the two girls did get into the secret room. I can imagine that they will explore the trunk for days to come.

PARTNER COMMENTS

I liked how your story seemed like a mystery. I liked the characters too. You made them come alive with what they did. Hannah even talked to Maria. I know they'll have fun with the trunk.

Read the fictional narrative and the comments that follow. Think about why this story scored a 3.

The Lost Book

Hannah looked for a book. Her friend Maria was visiting that afternoon. She wanted Maria to read this book.

Hannah looked but couldnt find the book. Was it in the closet? She looked in there. She could not see very much because it was dark. She uses a flashlight. She saw a door. Hannah didnt know about it before.

Hannah and Maria pulled the door. It was stuck and wouldnt open. They thought it might be locked.

The girls looked around and found a key to the door and they opened the door and went into a room. It really smelled. It was hard to see. They finally saw a trunk way over in the corner.

Maria new they would have fun exploring the trunk. It was better than the book.

Your Turn

Now it's your turn to help the writer. Find and fix the errors in the fictional narrative. Go back to the pages in green if you need help.

1. Find and fix the **paragraph** that is not indented. See pp. 56–57.
2. Find and fix the three **contraction** errors. See pp. 52–53.
3. Find and fix the **verb** that shows the incorrect time. See pp. 16–17.
4. Find and fix the **run-on sentence**. See pp. 44–45.
5. Find and fix the incorrect **homophone**. See pp. 36–37.

TEACHER COMMENTS

▲ Can you think of a title that tells more about the story?
▲ Your story has a beginning, middle, and ending, but I'd like more details.
▲ Having Hannah and Maria talk to each other would help to liven up your story.
▲ You might try to use more **exact words**. See pp. 26–27 and 32–33 for help.
▲ **Join** some short **sentences**. See pp. 42–43.

PARTNER COMMENTS

Your title gave me the wrong idea. I wanted to know more about Hannah and Maria. It was a pretty interesting story anyway.

Score: 2

Read the fictional narrative and the comments that follow. Think about why this story scored a 2.

1

The Closet

It was an old room. hannah looked for a book. Maria was her friend. She wood give the book to Maria to read. She put a light in her closet. She could not see because it was dark and dusty there was a door. Hannah and Maria pulled on the door and then pushed. The door was locked. They lookd behind old boxes. Then Hannah reached up and seen a key. She opened the door There was a room. Hannah and Maria saw a trunk. The trunk were better than the book. They new it

2

Your Turn

Now it's your turn to help the writer. Find and fix the errors in the fictional narrative. Go back to the pages in green if you need help.

1. Indent the **paragraph**. See pp. 56–57.
2. Find and fix the **capitalization** error. See pp. 46–47.
3. Find and fix the two incorrect **homophones**. See pp. 36–37.
4. Find and fix the **run-on sentence**. See pp. 44–45.
5. Find and fix the two incorrect **verbs** in the past. See pp. 16–19.
6. Find and fix the two errors in **end punctuation**. See pp. 38–39.
7. Find and fix the error in **subject-verb agreement**. See pp. 24–25.

TEACHER COMMENTS

4

▲ This story isn't just about the closet. You should write a title that tells more about the story.
▲ You mention the room at the beginning of the story, but you don't give any information about it until later on. This detail is out of order.
▲ More details about the closet, the girls, and the room would make the story more interesting.
▲ You need to break up your thoughts with separate paragraphs. Remember to indent.
▲ Use more **exact words**. See pp. 26–27 and 32–33 for help.
▲ Use more **sentence variety**. See pp. 38–39 and 60–61.

PARTNER COMMENTS

3

Your title didn't tell me what the story is about. The plot would have been better if you hadn't mentioned the room until the end. The events were hard for me to follow.

Read the fictional narrative and the comments that follow. Think about why this story scored a 1.

Two girls was Hannah and Maria. Hannah had a book. Hannah had a room with a closet. The girls looked in They seen it was dark in there. They pushed the door. Then there was a room. There was dust and things and a trunk two. hannah knowed the trunk wasnt knew. Her grandmothers name was anna. She was Anna Littlefield. It is all part of a long story. About that trunk. Now they do not need that book.

PARTNER COMMENTS

2

Your story didn't have a title, but that was just the first of the problems! You made too many errors. I couldn't follow the story.

TEACHER COMMENTS

3

▲ Can you think of a good title for your story?
▲ Try to think of ways to grab the reader's attention in the beginning and in the ending.
▲ I'd like more information about the setting.
▲ I have some trouble following the events in the story. Why did Hannah and Maria look in the closet?
▲ Make Hannah and Maria seem more real by having them talk to each other.
▲ Use some **variety** in your **sentences**. See pp. 38–39 and 60–61 for help.
▲ Use more **interesting words** to make your story more lively. See pp. 26–27 and 32–33.

4

Your Turn

Now it's your turn to help the writer. Find and fix the errors in the fictional narrative. Go back to the pages in green if you need help.

1. Indent the **paragraph**. See pp. 56–57.
2. Find and fix the error in **subject-verb agreement**. See pp. 24–25.
3. Find and fix the error in **end punctuation**. See pp. 38–39.
4. Find and fix the two incorrect past-time **verbs**. See pp. 18–19.
5. Find and fix the two incorrect **homophones**. See pp. 36–37.
6. Find and fix the two **capitalization** errors. See pp. 46–47.
7. Find and fix the **contraction** error. See pp. 52–53.
8. Find and fix the incorrect **possessive noun**. See pp. 8–9.
9. Find and fix the **sentence fragment**. See pp. 40–41.

USING A RUBRIC TO SCORE FICTIONAL NARRATIVES

This rubric is based on a point scale of 1 to 4. It was used to score the fictional narratives on pages 98–101. Use this rubric to remember what is important in fictional narratives.

4 A score of 4 means that the writer

- connects the writing directly to the prompt.
- almost always uses the correct forms of words.
- almost always uses capitalization and punctuation correctly.
- almost always uses clear and complete sentences and includes variety in sentences.
- includes interesting words.
- creates an attention-getting title that relates to the story.
- creates a clear beginning, middle, and ending.
- develops a clear setting, one or more interesting characters, and an active plot.
- uses some dialogue to make the characters come alive.
- begins a new paragraph for each change of idea or speaker.

2 A score of 2 means that the writer

- connects the writing to the prompt in a general way.
- uses some incorrect forms of words and some incorrect capitalization or punctuation.
- includes little variety in sentences and uses some run-on sentences or sentence fragments.
- includes mostly simple words.
- creates a title that relates somewhat to the story.
- creates a weak beginning, middle, or ending.
- fails to clearly develop a setting, characters, or a plot.
- uses little or no dialogue.
- makes some paragraphing errors.

3 A score of 3 means that the writer

- connects the writing to the prompt.
- usually uses the correct forms of words.
- usually uses capitalization and punctuation correctly.
- usually uses clear and complete sentences and includes some variety in sentences.
- includes some interesting words.
- creates a title that relates generally to the story.
- creates a beginning, middle, and ending.
- develops a setting, one or more characters, and a plot.
- may use some dialogue among characters.
- usually begins a new paragraph for each change of idea or speaker.

1 A score of 1 means that the writer

- does not successfully connect the writing to the prompt.
- uses many incorrect forms of words and often uses incorrect capitalization or punctuation.
- includes almost no variety in sentences and uses several run-on sentences or sentence fragments.
- uses simple words.
- creates a poor title or has no title at all.
- creates an unclear beginning, middle, or ending.
- fails to present or develop a setting, characters, or a plot.
- does not use dialogue or uses it incorrectly.
- makes paragraphing errors.

SCORING FICTIONAL NARRATIVES

Now it's your turn to score some fictional narratives. The four stories on pages 103 and 104 were written in response to this prompt.

Write a story about something that could never really happen.

Read each fictional narrative. Write a few comments about it. Then give it a score from 1 to 4. Think about what you've learned in this lesson as you match each story with its correct score.

Model A

Score:

homework

A mouse named Miranda went to the library Her friend was a lizard named lyza. The lizard had some paper. Lyza said that the paper was special. It could do homework. A moose calld Michael gave her the paper.

Miranda used the paper and it was different colors and it was warm. She could do math now. Her and Lyza was done. In no time. Miranda looked at a big pile of homework. It was all finished

then the mouse thought she would not use the lizards special paper. She told Lyza why.

Comments: _____
_____
_____
_____
_____
_____
_____
_____

Model B

Score:

A mouse and a lizard was friends. Went to the library. They bringed their homework. the lizard had some paper. Not like most paper. The paper turnd funny colors. There was writing on it The mouse and her friend did there work right away. The teacher wood be happy. The mouse told the lizard not to use the paper and she said the paper was a bad idea and you wont learn anything new with this paper

Comments: _____
_____
_____
_____
_____
_____
_____

Model C

Score:

The Unusual Paper

One afternoon a mouse named Miranda and a lizard named Lyza sat in the library. Lyza gave Miranda a piece of paper. Miranda started her homework. She wrote one sentence on the paper. Then the paper turned blue and yellow.

"What kind of paper is this? asked Miranda. Her report was all written!

"I got this unusual paper from a moose called Michael," said Lyza.

"Im so glad. I have to do my math next," Miranda said.

Miranda started her math homework. The paper turned pink and orange. The work was done. Miranda smiled. Then she frowned.

"Lyza, the paper does all the work. We won't learn anything on our own," Miranda said. Miranda decided to save the special paper for writing lists, notes, and letters. She would do her homework on regular paper.

Comments: _____

Model D

Score:

Lyza and Miranda

A mouse called Miranda and a lizard called Lyza were in the library. It was quiet. They started there homework. Lyza gave her friend a piece of paper. Miranda wrote on it and the paper turned different colors and then sentences showed up on their own.

"Where did you get this paper?" Miranda asked.

Lyza said that Michael the moose gave it to her. Miranda finished her report in one minute. Math was next. Miranda did one problem. She new the paper would do the rest. Then Miranda stopped. She told Lyza the special paper was fun but it wouldnt help her learn. Miranda then did her homework on her own.

Comments: _____

WRITING A FICTIONAL NARRATIVE

Now you get to write your own fictional narrative. Use the prompt below.

> *Write a story that you make up from your imagination.*

When You Write Your Fictional Narrative

1. **Think about** what you want to write. Ask yourself some questions.
   - Where and when will the story take place?
   - Who will be in the story?
   - What problem will the characters have to deal with?
   - How will the characters try to solve the problem?
   - What will be the result?

   Use graphic organizers to gather and sort your information.

2. **Write** your first draft. Be sure your fictional narrative has a clear beginning, middle, and ending. Your story can be imaginary, but it must always make sense.

3. **Read** your draft. Use the checklist that your teacher will give you to review your writing.

4. **Edit** your story. Make changes until your story reads well.

5. **Proofread** your story one last time.

6. **Write** a neat copy of your story and give it to your partner.

Work with a Partner

7. **Read** your partner's fictional narrative.

8. **Score** your partner's story from 1 to 4, using the rubric on page 102. Then complete the Partner Comments sheet that your teacher will give you. Tell what you liked about the story and what you think would make it better.

9. **Switch** papers.

10. **Think about** your partner's comments. Read your story again. Make any changes that you think will improve your fictional narrative.

11. **Write** a neat final copy of your fictional narrative.

Making Connections

- Have you ever heard a story that you wished had a different ending? Make up a new ending of your own. Write the story with your new ending.

- When you read about a past event in social studies, think about how that event could be written as a realistic story. What would the setting be? Who would the characters be? What would the problem be? Would you include art with the story? What would the art be?

- TV and movie characters may seem real because you can see them. Still, they must be developed through what they say, what they do, and how the other characters feel about them. Think about this the next time you watch your favorite program.

EXPOSITORY ESSAYS

Often you write an essay, or short paper, to explain something. The paper is called an expository essay. The examples and facts that you use often come from what you already know about the topic. Here is a sample writing prompt for an expository essay.

Write an essay that explains how to be a good listener.

Read the expository essay. It was written in response to the prompt. Then read the Writing Tips to learn more about expository essays.

Writing Tips

✳ Get your readers' interest right away. Make sure you include a sentence that states the topic in the first paragraph of your essay.

✳ The middle, or body, of your essay should include examples and facts that develop the topic. Include three or more main ideas about the topic. Each main idea should have its own paragraph. Each paragraph should have two or more details that back up that main idea. Do not include details that don't tell about the main idea.

✳ It's all right to express a few opinions about the topic, but stick mostly to examples or facts.

✳ Present your ideas in an order that makes sense.

✳ Make sure your last paragraph, or conclusion, wraps up the ideas in the essay.

How to Be a Good Listener

Imagine that you are sitting in an audience. Suddenly, everyone except you laughs. You have to ask the person next to you what the speaker said. A good listener wouldn't have to ask.

Here's how to be a good listener. First, give the speaker all your attention. Pretend that the speaker is talking only to you. This can help you tune into the speaker's words. It can help you tune out noise around you.

Next, sit still as you listen. Don't wiggle around, or you won't be able to listen very well. You might keep others from listening too.

Finally, keep your eye on the speaker. Watch the speaker's face and hands. You can get clues about the message.

Be a good listener. Then when everyone laughs, you'll laugh too.

USING GRAPHIC ORGANIZERS

Before you write, use graphic organizers. They can help you think about, gather, and sort information for your expository essay. The person who wrote the essay on page 106 might have used a Topic Web, such as the one below.

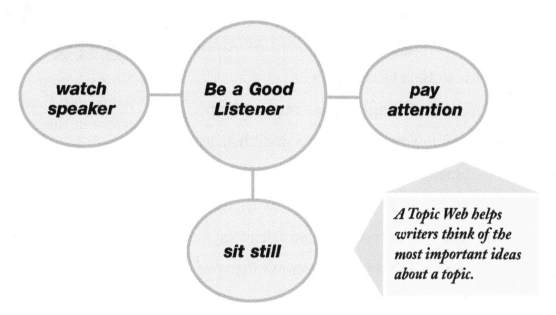

A Topic Web helps writers think of the most important ideas about a topic.

A Sequence Chart is also useful. It helps writers put their ideas in an order that makes sense. Look again at the essay on page 106. Use a few words to fill in each box in this Sequence Chart.

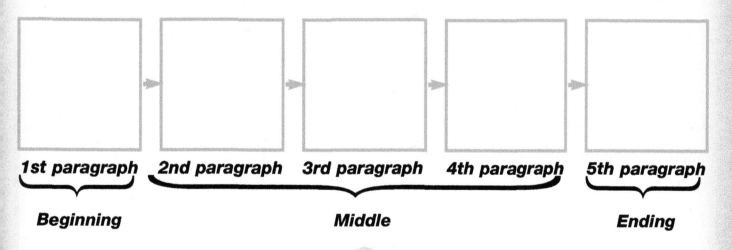

| 1st paragraph | 2nd paragraph | 3rd paragraph | 4th paragraph | 5th paragraph |

Beginning   **Middle**   **Ending**

A Sequence Chart helps writers put ideas in order.

Score: **4**

Read the expository essay below. It was written in response to the prompt on page 106. Next, read the comments and think about why this essay scored a 4.

1

How to Be a Good Listener

Listening is more than hearing. Listening can help you learn. Here are a few tips for being a good listener.

A friend has something to tell you. Give your full attention to your friend. Look directly at your friend. Dont daydream. Listen to everything your friend says. Nod your head from time to time. This shows that you are paying attention.

Think about what your friend is saying. Ask questions if you don't understand. You can ask right away if there is a pause. You may have to wait until your friend stops speaking, though.

Be polite. Don't interrupt. Wait until it's clear that your friend is done. Then you can give opinions or ask questions. Also, let your friend know that you appreciate the information.

Use these simple tips, and you'll become a good listener. You can learn a lot to.

Your Turn

Now it's your turn to help the writer. Find and fix the errors in the expository essay. Go back to the pages in green if you need help.

1. Find and fix the **contraction** error. See pp. 52–53.

2. Find and fix the incorrect **homophone**. See pp. 36–37.

TEACHER COMMENTS

4

▲ I like how you get my attention right away and then state your topic.
▲ The organization of your essay is clear, with a new paragraph for each new idea.
▲ You present your ideas in an order that makes sense.
▲ You include strong details to support each main idea.
▲ I like the variety you use in your sentences.
▲ The last paragraph clearly wraps up the essay.

PARTNER COMMENTS

2

3

You got my attention right away. I understood your listening tips. You tied up the ideas at the end. You explained how to be a good listener.

Read the expository essay and the comments that follow. Think about why this essay scored a 3.

1

Listening

It is important to be a good listener. You can learn a lot. Here are three tips for being a good listener.

Pretend your friend has something to say. You should pay attention. Look right at your friend. Dont think about other things. You can nod your head. This shows you are listening.

Do you understand what your friend is saying You can ask questions. Sometimes you can ask right away. Sometimes you should wait.

Don't break in. Let your friend keep on talking. It is your friends' turn. It's not polite to interrupt. Wait until your friend is threw. Then you can say what is on your mind

These are the three things to remember. For being a good listener. You might learn something too.

Your Turn

Now it's your turn to help the writer. Find and fix the errors in the expository essay. Go back to the pages in green if you need help.

1. Find and fix the **contraction** error. See pp. 52–53.
2. Find and fix the two errors in **end punctuation**. See pp. 38–39.
3. Find and fix the incorrect **possessive noun**. See pp. 8–9.
4. Find and fix the incorrect **homophone**. See pp. 36–37.
5. Find and fix the **sentence fragment**. See pp. 40–41.

TEACHER COMMENTS

4

▲ Try to begin your essay in a way that will encourage readers to read more.

▲ Good job organizing your essay. You introduce the topic, give your main ideas, and then wrap up the ideas in the last paragraph.

▲ Use more **exact words**. See pp. 26–27 and 32–33 for help.

▲ Use more variety in **sentences**. See pp. 39–39 and 60–61.

PARTNER COMMENTS

2

Your essay was organized well enough. I understood the tips OK. Your sentences were a little choppy, though.

3

Score:

2

Read the expository essay and the comments that follow. Think about why this essay scored a 2.

1

Listening can help. You might learn something if you listen. Hear is how.

Say a friend has something to say. It is good to listen carefully. Do not look at other things. do look at your friend. You can nod, but do not go to sleep Do not daydream. Do not walk away.

You can ask questions. When you want. This tells your Friend that you are listening. Make sure you understands what your friend says.

Your friend maked the time to talk. You should listen up. You might learn something

Your Turn

Now it's your turn to help the writer. Find and fix the errors in the expository essay. Go back to the pages in green if you need help.

1. Find and fix the incorrect **homophone**. See pp. 36–37.
2. Find and fix the two errors in **capitalization**. See pp. 46–47.
3. Find and fix the two errors in **end punctuation**. See pp. 38–39.
4. Find and fix the **paragraph** that is not indented. See pp. 56–57.
5. Find and fix the **sentence fragment**. See pp. 40–41.
6. Find and fix the error in **subject-verb agreement**. See pp. 22–23.
7. Find and fix the **past-time verb** that is incorrect. See pp. 18–19.

2

PARTNER COMMENTS

Your essay is clearly about listening, and your thoughts are somewhat in order. You have lots of short sentences, though, and too many begin the same way.

3

TEACHER COMMENTS

4

▲ Can you think of a good title for your essay?
▲ Good job letting me know what your topic is and beginning a new paragraph for each main idea.
▲ You could add more details to support the main ideas. See pp. 58–59 for help.
▲ **Join** some **short sentences** to make longer sentences. See pp. 42–43.
▲ You should use some variety among your **sentences.** See pp. 38–39 and 60–61.

Score:

Read the expository essay and the comments that follow. Think about why this essay scored a 1.

My brother talks all the time. To say he talks a lot hardly says it He talks about school. He talks about ball games he talks about his buddys. He talks about wishs too. He talks about everything. Does he ever listen He never listens. who listens? He talks to my mother sometimes. He and her talk a lot. Does she listen? All the time. She had a cold last week. then she could not listen. He asked me. I knowed better. I left. Why should I listen?

PARTNER COMMENTS

2

You didn't follow the prompt. Your essay was about your brother. It didn't explain how to be a good listener. I did learn a lot about your brother, though.

TEACHER COMMENTS

3

▲ Be sure you understand what the prompt is asking before you start to write. You didn't follow this prompt.

▲ Your essay needs a title. What's a good one?

▲ Though you tell me a lot about your brother, your ideas wander. Whatever the topic, choose some important ideas and back them up with details. Have a clear beginning, middle, and ending.

▲ Use **paragraphs** to separate your thoughts.
See pp. 56–57 for help.

▲ Use some different kinds of **sentences**. Many of your sentences start with the word *he*.
See pp. 38–39 and 60–61.

Your Turn

Now it's your turn to help the writer. Find and fix the errors in the expository essay. Go back to the pages in green if you need help.

1. Indent the **paragraph**.
See pp. 56–57.

2. Find and fix the two **end punctuation** errors.
See pp. 38–39.

3. Find and fix the **run-on sentence**.
See pp. 44–45.

4. Find and fix the two incorrect **plural nouns**.
See pp. 6–7.

5. Find and fix the two **capitalization** errors.
See pp. 46–47.

6. Find and fix the incorrect **pronoun**.
See pp. 12–13.

7. Find and fix the **sentence fragment**.
See pp. 40–41.

8. Find and fix the incorrect **past-time verb**.
See pp. 16–19.

4

USING A RUBRIC TO SCORE EXPOSITORY ESSAYS

This rubric is based on a point scale of 1 to 4. It was used to score the expository essays on pages 108–111. Use this rubric to remember what is important in expository essays.

4 A score of 4 means that the writer

- connects the writing directly to the prompt.
- almost always uses the correct forms of words.
- almost always uses capitalization and punctuation correctly.
- almost always uses clear and complete sentences and includes variety in sentences.
- includes effective words.
- creates a title that relates directly to the topic.
- introduces the topic clearly at the beginning.
- creates a clear beginning, middle, and ending.
- explains the topic with at least three main ideas, along with supporting details.
- puts the ideas in an order that creates a strong and clear essay.
- begins a new paragraph for each change of idea.

2 A score of 2 means that the writer

- connects the writing to the prompt in a general way.
- uses some incorrect forms of words and some incorrect capitalization or punctuation.
- includes little variety in sentences and uses some run-on sentences or sentence fragments.
- includes mostly simple words.
- creates a title that relates somewhat to the topic.
- presents the topic within the essay but uses too few main ideas or details to explain the topic fully.
- creates a weak beginning, middle, or ending.
- puts the ideas in a weak or choppy order.
- makes some paragraphing errors.

3 A score of 3 means that the writer

- connects the writing to the prompt.
- usually uses the correct forms of words.
- usually uses capitalization and punctuation correctly.
- usually uses clear and complete sentences and includes some variety in sentences.
- includes some effective words.
- creates a title that relates to the topic.
- introduces the topic toward the beginning.
- creates a beginning, middle, and ending.
- explains the topic with some main ideas, along with some supporting details.
- puts the ideas in an order that makes sense.
- usually begins a new paragraph for each change of idea.

1 A score of 1 means that the writer

- does not successfully connect the writing to the prompt.
- uses many incorrect forms of words and often uses incorrect capitalization or punctuation.
- includes almost no variety in sentences and uses several run-on sentences or sentence fragments.
- includes only simple words.
- creates a poor title or has no title at all.
- includes the topic in the essay but uses too few main ideas or details to explain the topic.
- creates an unclear beginning, middle, or ending.
- puts the ideas in an unclear order.
- makes paragraphing errors.

SCORING EXPOSITORY ESSAYS

Now it's your turn to score some expository essays. The four essays on pages 113 and 114 were written in response to this prompt.

> *Write an essay about someone you find interesting.*

Read each expository essay. Write a few comments about it. Then give it a score from 1 to 4. Think about what you've learned in this lesson as you match each essay with its correct score.

Model A

Score: ▽

What do I know about Helen keller. An interesting person. She could here when she was young. Then she couldnt. She was sick. She had a teacher. Named miss Sullivan. she was hard. Her and Helen did a lot. She went to college. She worked hard and she did a lot of work and she seen a lot of people. People liked her. I think shes the interesting one. The end.

Comments: _____

_____

_____

_____

_____

_____

_____

_____

_____

Model B

Score: ▽

Helen Keller

One of the most interesting people I know about is Helen Keller. She had a hard start in life. She didnt let it stop her, though.

Helen was born a long time ago. She got sick when she was very young. Helen got better, but she could no longer see or hear. She acted up. Helen's parents hired a teacher named Anne Sullivan. Miss Sullivan was calm and strong. She could handle Helen. She taught Helen a lot about language.

Helen learned to speak, write, and read. She went to college. She became a famous writer and speaker. I think she was brave and interesting.

Comments: _____

_____

_____

_____

_____

_____

_____

Model C

Score:

The Interesting Person
Helen Keller is the interesting person. I think shes very interesting.

She could see and here when she was little. Then she couldnt because she got sick. She still couldn't when she got better.
She got a teacher. Her teacher taught her to do a lot and to no words. She spelld words. Then she learnd to do a lot more. Her teacher was kind She went to College. It was hard. people liked Helen a lot. Helen keller was very interesting.

Comments: _____
_____
_____
_____
_____
_____
_____
_____

Model D

Score:

Interesting Helen Keller
Helen Keller was a very interesting person. I read about her.

Helen could see and hear when she was young. Then she got sick, and she couldn't see or here anymore. Then Helen was wild and out of control. Her parents got a teacher for her. The teachers name was Miss Sullivan. Her teacher wasn't mean. She wasn't easy either. Helen learned a lot.

Helen learned more and more. She learned to speak and write and read. Enough to go to college. Helen became famous.

Helen Keller had to work hard. She did. It worked for her. I think she shows what you can do if your willing to work. That's why I'm writing about her.

Comments: _____
_____
_____
_____
_____
_____
_____
_____

WRITING AN EXPOSITORY ESSAY

Now you get to write your own expository essay. Use the prompt below.

> *Think about something that you do well. Write an essay that explains how to do it.*

When You Write Your Expository Essay

1. **Think about** what you want to write. Ask yourself what you know about the topic.

   - What are the most important ideas about the topic?
   - What details can I add to support the main ideas?

   Use graphic organizers to gather and sort your information.

2. **Write** your first draft. Be sure your essay has a clear beginning, middle, and ending.

3. **Read** your draft. Use the checklist that your teacher will give you to review your writing.

4. **Edit** your essay. Make changes until your essay reads well.

5. **Proofread** your essay one last time.

6. **Write** a neat copy of your essay and give it to your partner.

Work with a Partner

7. **Read** your partner's expository essay.

8. **Score** your partner's essay from 1 to 4, using the rubric on page 112. Then complete the Partner Comments sheet that your teacher will give you. Tell what you liked about the essay and what you think would make it better.

9. **Switch** papers.

10. **Think about** your partner's comments. Read your essay again. Make any changes that you think will improve your expository essay.

11. **Write** a neat final copy of your expository essay.

Making Connections

- Has anyone ever given you an explanation or a set of directions, but you really have no idea what it's all about? Think about what makes explanations or directions easy or difficult to follow. Keep your ideas in mind when you give explanations or directions to other people.

- Listen to a TV news story. Does the story tell you what happened? Whom it happened to? When, where, and why it happened? Knowing the answers to questions such as these can help you with expository writing.

An opinion is what you think or feel about something. You probably have thoughts and feelings about many things. When you express these thoughts and feelings in writing, you are writing an opinion. In an opinion, you try to make the reader see that you are right. Here is a sample writing prompt for an opinion.

> *Write your opinion on whether a skunk would make a good pet.*

Read the opinion. It was written in response to the prompt. Then read the Writing Tips to learn more about opinions.

Writing Tips

* It's easiest to convince readers to agree with your opinion about topics that you know well. What you know may come from your experiences or from your reading.

* Introduce the topic and your opinion of it at the beginning. Sometimes it helps to state the topic as a question.

* Provide strong reasons to back up your opinion. Support each reason with facts and examples.

* Use strong, clear words.

* Be forceful, but don't be rude. Remember, you want to change minds, not hurt feelings.

* End strong. State one of your strongest reasons or facts last.

Why Skunks Don't Make Good Pets

Skunks are wild animals, and they should stay in the wild. Skunks should not be pets.

All skunks are curious, and they like to roam around. A caged skunk would be sad because it would be alone and it couldn't move around.

Skunks must eat many kinds of food. Skunks can get sick if they don't get the various kinds of food that they need.

Remember, skunks are not like cats or dogs. Skunks may bite when they are upset, and they do not come when you call them. Skunks do not do tricks.

A pet skunk has to stay a pet. You can't release a pet skunk into the wild again. It would have no defense against enemies, and it would not know how to find food or shelter.

Pet skunks can suffer because people do not know the right way to take care of them. I think that skunks should be in the wild because it's the best home for them.

USING GRAPHIC ORGANIZERS

Before you write, use graphic organizers. They can help you think about, gather, and sort the information for your opinion. The person who wrote the opinion on page 116 might have used an Opinion Chart, such as the one below.

What is the topic?
Do skunks make good pets?

What is your opinion?
Skunks don't make good pets.

An Opinion Chart helps writers think about their opinion and the reasons and facts that back it up.

What reasons or facts back up your opinion?			
Skunks like to roam.	**Skunks need various foods.**	**Skunks aren't like cats or dogs.**	**Pet skunks can't go back into the wild.**

A Reasons and Facts Chart can also be helpful for gathering facts or examples that support a key reason for an opinion. How might the writer of the opinion on page 116 have used this chart? Fill in the empty boxes.

Skunks aren't like cats or dogs.

A Reasons and Facts Chart helps writers organize information for an opinion. In the main box, writers jot down one reason that backs up their opinion. In the other boxes, they add supporting facts or examples.

Score: **4**

Read the opinion below. It was written in response to the prompt on page 116. Next, read the comments and think about why this opinion scored a 4.

1

Skunks Make Great Pets

A skunk is good company and a good pet. How do I know? I own a pet skunk, Stinky.

Stinky doesn't really smell bad. All pet skunks have their scent glands removeed. That way, they can't spray anymore. Skunks groom themselves and enjoy taking baths. They can also be trained to use a litter box like cats.

Skunks are smart. You can teach them to do just about anything. Just make sure you give them a reward.

Pet skunks are fun. Stinky loves to play with me. We roll on the floor and we play tug-of-war. Skunks are cuddly too. Stinky used to sleep tucked inside my shirt. Now he likes to curl around my neck.

The best part is that skunks live long lives. Pet skunks can live to be 15 years old. Stinky could be my pet for a long time!

Your Turn

Now it's your turn to help the writer. Find and fix the errors in the opinion. Go back to the pages in green if you need help.

1. Find and fix the **verb** that shows past time incorrectly. See pp. 16–17.

2. Find and fix the missing **comma** when joining two sentences with the word **and**. See pp. 42–43.

TEACHER COMMENTS

4

▲ Your title is a good clue to your opinion.

▲ Your opening sentence immediately draws me in. All in all, your beginning is quite strong.

▲ You've done a great job trying to get the reader to agree with your opinion. Your reasons are clear, and you provide strong details to support them.

▲ Your writing is easy to read. You have organized your ideas well.

▲ Your word choices and sentences have variety. This makes your writing fun for readers.

▲ I like how you end with the strongest reason for having a pet skunk! Nice job!

PARTNER COMMENTS

2

3

Your beginning is terrific! I could tell how you feel about having a pet skunk. You gave good reasons for your opinion.

Read the opinion and the comments that follow. Think about why this opinion scored a 3.

Pet Skunks

A skunk can make a great pet. I like my pet skunk. Stinky is his name.

Stinkys scent glands were taken out before he was sold. Now he cant spray any smelly juice. Stinky grooms himself. He likes to take baths. He uses a litter box. Skunks are smart animals. I taught stinky lots of tricks. He likes a reward first.

Stinky is fun to play with. Stinky and I roll on the floor together we also play tug-of-war. Skunks are cuddly too. Stinky liked to sleep inside my shirt as a baby. Now he likes to be around my neck.

Some skunks can live 15 years. that means that Stinky and me will be together a long time.

Your Turn

Now it's your turn to help the writer. Find and fix the errors in the opinion. Go back to the pages in green if you need help.

1. Find the fix the incorrect **possessive noun**. See pp. 8–9.
2. Find the fix the **contraction** error. See pp. 52–53.
3. Find and fix the two errors in **capitalization**. See pp. 46–47.
4. Find and fix the **run-on sentence**. See pp. 44–45.
5. Find and fix the incorrect **pronoun**. See pp. 12–13.

TEACHER COMMENTS

▲ It's easy to tell what your opinion is, and you've given lots of reasons to support it. Your reasons could be better connected, though.

▲ You've chosen some exact and colorful words. Please add a few more.

▲ Try for more **variety** in your **sentences**. See pp. 38–39 and 60–61 for help.

PARTNER COMMENTS

You gave your opinion in the first sentence. But too many of your sentences began with the words *Stinky* or *he*. At the end, you said the same thing twice.

Score: **2**

Read the opinion and the comments that follow. Think about why this opinion scored a 2.

1

Stinky

A skunk makes a good pet. My pet skunk is called stinky. Hes a good pet. I like him a lot.

Stinky smells OK. He cant spray any smelly stuff. Stinky is smart. he can do lots of things. He is bad sometimes. Opens doors and dumps out stuff. I have to yell at him. Stinky is lots of fun. We roll on the floor we play tug-of-war with his toys.

Do you think all skunks are black and white That is not true. They can be brown or gray. They can't be purple or yellow. They can have spots to. A pet skunk can live a long time It makes a good pet.

Your Turn

Now it's your turn to help the writer. Find and fix the errors in the opinion. Go back to the pages in green if you need help.

1. Find and fix the two errors in **capitalization**. See pp. 46–49.
2. Find and fix the two **contraction** errors. See pp. 52–53.
3. Find and fix the **sentence fragment**. See pp. 40–41.
4. Find and fix the **run-on sentence**. See pp. 44–45.
5. Find and fix the two **end punctuation** errors. See pp. 38–39.
6. Find and fix the incorrect **homophone**. See pp. 36–37.
7. Find and fix the **paragraph** that is not indented. See pp. 56–57.

2

PARTNER COMMENTS

You wrote a description, not an opinion. You said that a skunk makes a good pet, but the details don't always go with this opinion.

3

4

TEACHER COMMENTS

▲ You state your opinion clearly at the start, but then your writing wanders. You've included several details that do not belong. I suggest that you replace the sentences describing the colors of skunks with more reasons to support your opinion.

▲ Sometimes you say the same thing twice. Can you find the places where you repeat yourself?

▲ You have many short sentences. **Join** some of them into longer **sentences**. See pp. 42–43 for help.

▲ Try to make better **word choices**. See pp. 26–27 and 32–33.

Read the opinion and the comments that follow.
Think about why this opinion scored a 1.

I have a pet skunk. Stinky is my pet skunk. Stinky is black and white he has a fluffy tail. Stinky and me play all the time. we play a lot. My cat and Stinky are friends to. My cats name is Cool. Stinky is strong. He opens things. He always get into trouble. Stinky has sharp teeth but doesnt bite. He wood never hurt me. Stinky does tricks. I taught Stinky to stand up. To beg for food. stinky likes to be held. I hold him a lot. He is smart. Hes nice.

PARTNER COMMENTS

2

You didn't write an opinion. Mostly you described Stinky. You gave lots of details, but you didn't put them in order.

TEACHER COMMENTS

3

▲ You need a title. Think of a title that gives the reader a clue about your opinion.

▲ Did you forget what you were supposed to write? You never state your opinion directly.

▲ You've mostly written a list of details that describe Stinky. You should focus on reasons that Stinky makes a good pet.

▲ Your sentences have no order. You should have arranged them in a better way.

▲ Try not to repeat **details**. See pp. 58–59 for help.

▲ Can you **join** a few of the short **sentences** into longer sentences? See pp. 42–43.

Your Turn

4

Now it's your turn to help the writer. Find and fix the errors in the opinion. Go back to the pages in green if you need help.

1. Indent the **paragraph**. See pp. 56–57.

2. Find and fix the **run-on sentence**. See pp. 44–45.

3. Find and fix the incorrect **pronoun**. See pp. 12–13.

4. Find and fix the two errors in **capitalization**. See pp. 46–49.

5. Find and fix the two incorrect **homophones**. See pp. 36–37.

6. Find and fix the incorrect **possessive noun**. See pp. 8–9.

7. Find and fix the error in **subject-verb agreement**. See pp. 22–23.

8. Find and fix the two **contraction** errors. See pp. 52–53.

9. Find and fix the **sentence fragment**. See pp. 40–41.

USING A RUBRIC TO SCORE OPINIONS

This rubric is based on a point scale of 1 to 4. It was used to score the opinions on pages 118–121. Use this rubric to remember what is important in opinions.

4 A score of 4 means that the writer
- connects the writing directly to the prompt.
- almost always uses the correct forms of words.
- almost always uses capitalization and punctuation correctly.
- almost always writes clear and complete sentences and includes variety in sentences.
- includes clear, strong words.
- creates a title that relates directly to the topic.
- clearly introduces the topic and an opinion at the beginning.
- creates a clear beginning, middle, and ending.
- backs up the opinion with strong reasons and facts.
- puts the reasons in an order that creates a strong and clear opinion.
- begins a new paragraph for each new reason.

2 A score of 2 means that the writer
- connects the writing to the prompt in a general way.
- uses some incorrect forms of words and some incorrect capitalization or punctuation.
- includes little variety in sentences and uses some run-on sentences or sentence fragments.
- includes mostly simple words.
- creates a title that relates only somewhat to the topic.
- creates a weak beginning, middle, or ending.
- provides too few reasons or facts to back up the opinion.
- puts reasons in a weak or choppy order.
- makes some paragraphing errors.

3 A score of 3 means that the writer
- connects the writing to the prompt.
- usually uses the correct forms of words.
- usually uses capitalization and punctuation correctly.
- usually uses clear and complete sentences and includes some variety in sentences.
- includes some effective words.
- creates a title that relates to the topic.
- introduces the topic and an opinion toward the beginning.
- creates a beginning, middle, and ending.
- backs up the opinion with some strong reasons and facts.
- puts the reasons in an order that makes sense.
- usually begins a new paragraph for each new reason.

1 A score of 1 means that the writer
- does not successfully connect the writing to the prompt.
- uses many incorrect forms of words.
- often uses incorrect capitalization or punctuation.
- includes almost no variety in sentences and uses several run-on sentences or sentence fragments.
- includes only simple words.
- creates a poor title or has no title at all.
- creates an unclear beginning, middle, or ending.
- fails to provide enough reasons or facts to back up the opinion.
- puts reasons in no particular order.
- makes paragraphing errors.

SCORING OPINIONS

Now it's your turn to score some opinions. The four opinions on pages 123 and 124 were written in response to this prompt.

> *Write your opinion about whether a raccoon makes a good pet.*

Read each opinion. Write a few comments about it. Then give it a score from 1 to 4. Think about what you've learned in this lesson as you match each opinion with its correct score.

Model A

Score: ▽

Raccoons

Raccoons cause tons of trouble. Dont want one in my house. Raccoons are pretty strong they like to poke into things. your things wont be safe because they get into them. Raccoons mess up stuff They tip over trash cans. Raccoons dig holes in your bed.

Hungry raccoons bug you a lot. Hungry raccoons eat and eat and get really fat. your raccoon can make you sick. why get a raccoon.

Comments: _____
_____
_____
_____
_____
_____
_____
_____
_____

Model B

Score: ▽

Troublemakers

Why would you want a raccoon? Raccoons cause lots of trouble. Raccoons are strong. They are nosy too. They like to poke into things. So raccoons get into things. Your stuff is not safe. Raccoons mess with backpacks and other things. They get into trash. They make large holes in your bed for a nest.

Hungry raccoons bug you until you feed them they are messy eaters. A raccoons meal has to be special.

Raccoons are tough to live with. They dont always make the best pet.

Comments: _____
_____
_____
_____
_____
_____
_____
_____

Model C

Score:

Raccoons dont make pets. Raccoons are pretty strong they poke in things. Your things arent safe. They get in them. Raccoons mess with stuff and they open doors and they take stuff. raccoons have sharp teeth. Raccoons bite. There claws four digging. Who needs it. Raccoons is a pain.

Comments: _____

_____

_____

_____

_____

_____

_____

Model D

Score:

A Pet Raccoon Spells Trouble

Why would anyone want to own a raccoon? A raccoon in the house can cause all kinds of trouble.

Raccoon are strong for their size and raccoons are curious. That means a raccoon can get into everything. Nothing you own will be safe. A raccoon will dump out backpacks and laundry baskets. It will open cabinets and drawers. Raccoons like to dig large holes in beds for nests.

A raccoon eats a lot, but you can't just give it any food. You have to prepare special meals so it wont get sick.

A raccoon is clearly not easy to care for. So it's not the pet for me.

Comments: _____

_____

_____

_____

_____

_____

_____

WRITING AN OPINION

Now you get to write your own opinion.
Use the prompt below.

> *Write your opinion on whether rainy days are good or bad.*

When You Write Your Opinion

1. **Think about** what you want to write. Ask yourself some questions.
   - What is my opinion?
   - Why do I think or feel that way?
   - What examples and facts can I use to support my opinion?

   Use graphic organizers to gather and sort your information.

2. **Write** your first draft. Let your ideas flow. Be sure your opinion has a clear beginning, middle, and ending.

3. **Read** your draft. Use the checklist that your teacher will give you to review your writing.

4. **Edit** your opinion. Make changes until you like the way your opinion sounds.

5. **Proofread** your opinion one last time.

6. **Write** a neat copy of your opinion and give it to your partner.

Work with a Partner

7. **Read** your partner's opinion.

8. **Score** your partner's opinion from 1 to 4, using the rubric on page 122. Then complete the Partner Comments sheet that your teacher will give you. Tell what you liked about the opinion and what you think would make it better.

9. **Switch** papers.

10. **Think about** your partner's comments. Read your opinion again. Make any changes that you think will improve your opinion.

11. **Write** a neat final copy of your opinion.

Making Connections

- As you read books or watch TV shows and movies, notice the opinions you form. You may feel that a character is behaving badly. You may also not agree with a choice that a character has made. A good place for you to share these opinions is your journal.

- Opinions appear in many kinds of writing. Look for opinions in ads, book and movie reviews, and letters in newspapers. In what other places can you find written opinions?

- As you listen to people talk, think about the different ways in which they express their opinions. Do they speak calmly, or do they shout? What manner do you think works better for convincing others that an opinion is right?

SUMMARIES

One way to know whether you have understood something you have read is to write a **summary**. A summary is a short piece of writing that tells the most important points of a longer piece of writing.

In a summary of nonfiction, you write the most important ideas. In a summary of fiction, you write about the most important characters and events.

Here is a sample prompt for writing a summary of a nonfiction passage.

> *Read the passage "Lion Prides" on page 127.*
> *Then write a one-paragraph summary of the passage.*

Read the passage on page 127. Next, read the summary of the passage below. It was written in response to the prompt. Then read the Writing Tips to learn more about summaries.

Writing Tips

❋ With a long passage that you are going to summarize, look for details that answer *who, what, when, where, why,* and *how* questions. These can guide you to the most important points in the reading passage.

❋ Sometimes nonfiction reading passages have words or headings printed in special type. You can use these as guides to the most important ideas.

❋ Most summaries should be one paragraph long.

❋ In a summary, use your own words whenever possible. It is all right to use some key terms from the main passage. However, don't copy large portions of text from the main passage.

❋ Keep the summary simple.

❋ Write the important ideas in the same order as they appear in the main passage.

❋ Don't add any new ideas to the summary.

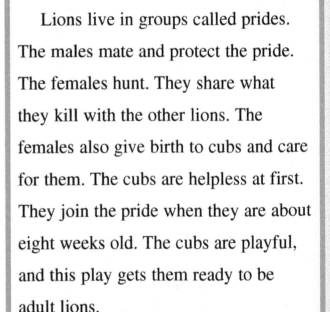

Lions live in groups called prides. The males mate and protect the pride. The females hunt. They share what they kill with the other lions. The females also give birth to cubs and care for them. The cubs are helpless at first. They join the pride when they are about eight weeks old. The cubs are playful, and this play gets them ready to be adult lions.

Here is the reading passage from which the summary on page 126 was written.

Lion Prides

Lions are huge wild cats that live mainly in the grasslands of Africa. Social animals, lions live together in groups called prides. A pride is like a team. The members of a pride have particular jobs.

Pride males have two main jobs. One is to mate with pride females to produce cubs. The other job of males is to protect the pride from enemies such as other lions. Male lions can weigh up to 500 pounds. They have strong muscles, sharp teeth, and sharply curved claws. Though pride males can often scare enemies away with a roar, they are willing to fight to the death to protect the females of the pride and their young.

Like males, pride females have two main jobs. One is to hunt. The females usually hunt at night. They stalk, or follow, their prey. The females hide in the tall grass, which is the same color as their light-brown fur. Then they leap on the prey and kill it with their sharp teeth. The females share the food with the rest of the pride. A pride female's other job is to give birth and raise lion cubs. A lion litter is usually two or three cubs. The cubs are blind and helpless at birth. The mother lion cares for the cubs until they are about eight weeks old, when they join the pride.

When the young cubs join the pride, they are very playful. Their play helps them develop new skills. As they wrestle, climb, chase, and explore, they are learning how to be adult lions.

Before you write, use graphic organizers. They can help you sort out the most important ideas for a summary.

The person who wrote the summary on page 126 about lion prides might have used a Topic Web, such as the one below.

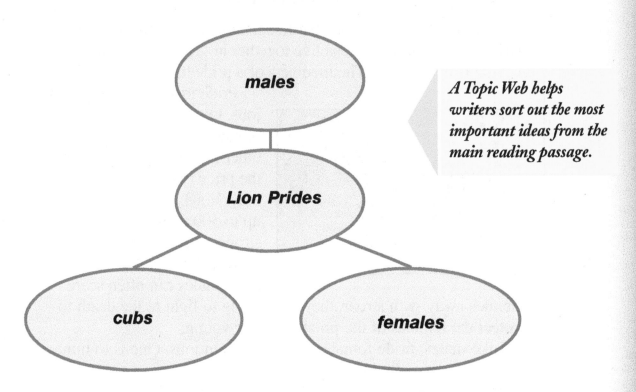

A Topic Web helps writers sort out the most important ideas from the main reading passage.

A Sequence Chart is helpful for putting the important ideas for a summary in the same order as they appear in the main passage. Fill in the chart below as if you were the writer of the summary on page 126.

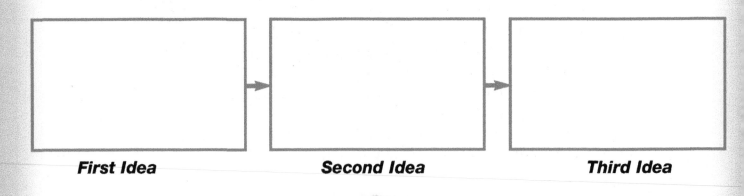

First Idea   **Second Idea**   **Third Idea**

A Sequence Chart helps writers put ideas in order.

Score: **4**

Read the summary below. It was written in response to the prompt on page 126. Next, read the comments and think about why this summary scored a 4.

1

Lions are big cats. They live together in groups called prides. Prides are something like teams. Lions in prides have special jobs. The male lions mate with the females so that there will be cubs. The males also protect the pride from enemys. The female lions hunt for food. They also raise lion cubs. The cubs are playful. Their play teaches them how to be adult lions.

Your Turn

Now it's your turn to help the writer. Find and fix the error in the summary. Go back to the pages in green if you need help.

1. Find and fix the incorrect **plural noun**. See pp. 6–7.

2

PARTNER COMMENTS

Your summary is short and clear. It told me what the longer reading passage is mostly about. You used simple words. You did not add any new ideas. You presented the ideas in the right order. It is a good summary.

3

TEACHER COMMENTS

4

▲ Your summary is the correct length.
▲ You mention the topic at the beginning of the summary. You also present the ideas in the same order as they are presented in the main reading passage. Good work!
▲ Your summary includes the most important ideas from the main passage. I can tell what the main passage is about by reading your summary. Thanks!
▲ Your word choice is clear and simple. You haven't used any language that takes away from the important ideas.
▲ Thank you for not adding any new information to the summary.

Score: 3

Read the summary and the comments that follow.
Think about why this summary scored a 3.

1

Lions live in Africa. There are not many lions in the united States. Lions live in prides. The lions in a pride have special jobs. The male lions produce cubs. The males also keep the pride safe. The female lions gets food and raise lion cubs. The cubs are very playful. They learn how to be adult lions

Your Turn

Now it's your turn to help the writer. Find and fix the errors in the summary. Go back to the pages in green if you need help.

1. Find and fix the **capitalization** error. See pp. 46–47.

2. Find and fix the error in **subject-verb agreement**. See pp. 22–23.

3. Find and fix the **end punctuation** error. See pp. 38–39.

2

PARTNER COMMENTS

Your summary is in order and gave me some idea of what the longer passage is about. One detail gives the wrong idea. (Do male lions really produce cubs?) You added a new detail, about lions in the United States. This doesn't belong in your summary.

3

TEACHER COMMENTS

4

▲ Your summary is a good length.
▲ Your summary includes many, but not all, of the most important ideas in the main passage.
▲ You use your own words most of the time. Good!
▲ The order of ideas follows the order in the main passage.
▲ Be careful! You have added information about lions in the United States, but this detail isn't in the main passage.
▲ One **detail** you included about male lions is a mistake. (Males alone do not produce cubs.)
See pp. 58–59 for help.

Read the summary and the comments that follow. Think about why this summary scored a 2.

Lions are huge wild cats that live in the grasslands of africa. They live together in groups called prides. A pride is like a team. The members have particular jobs.

Males are big and strong and grows curved claws. females are more small and light brown. Litters is small. Lion cubs are very playful and cute

Your Turn

Now it's your turn to help the writer. Find and fix the errors in the summary. Go back to the pages in green if you need help.

1. Find and fix the **paragraph** that is not indented. See pp. 56–57.
2. Find and fix the two **capitalization** errors. See pp. 46–47.
3. Find and fix the two errors in **subject-verb agreement**. See pp. 22–25.
4. Find and fix the incorrect **adjective that compares**. See pp. 30–31.
5. Find and fix the **end punctuation** error. See pp. 38–39.

PARTNER COMMENTS

Your first paragraph is mostly copied from the first paragraph of the original passage. The other details you gave are correct, but they aren't always important. The copying weakened your whole summary.

TEACHER COMMENTS

 Your summary gives some information about lion prides, but you often copied directly from the main passage. You should use your own words in a summary.

△ Your summary has two paragraphs. It should be one paragraph long.

△ You have included more unimportant information than important information in your summary.

△ You state that lion cubs are cute. That is your opinion. It is not in the main passage and should not be in the summary.

△ Not all the ideas in the summary follow the order of ideas in the main passage.

Score:

1

Read the summary and the comments that follow. Think about why this summary scored a 1.

1

Lions are big cats and they are brown and they hunt. They dont live in houses. They live in prides. They live in africa They all have jobs. there males and females and cubs. I think lion cubs are good four pets

PARTNER COMMENTS

2

Your summary doesn't include the most important ideas of the long passage. You also added details that don't belong. You began almost all of your sentences with the word *they*. This is not a good summary.

3

TEACHER COMMENTS

▲ Your summary is a good length, but it should tell more about lion prides.

▲ Your summary includes only a few important ideas from the main passage.

▲ It is your opinion that lion cubs make good pets. The summary should not include opinions.

▲ Your ideas do not all follow the order of ideas in the main passage.

Your Turn

Now it's your turn to help the writer. Find and fix the errors in the summary. Go back to the pages in green if you need help.

1. Indent the **paragraph**. See pp. 56–57.

2. Find and fix the **run-on sentence**. See pp. 44–45.

3. Find and fix the **contraction** error. See pp. 52–53.

4. Find and fix the two **capitalization** errors. See pp. 46–47.

5. Find and fix the two **end punctuation** errors. See pp. 38–39.

6. Find and fix the **sentence fragment**. See pp. 40–41.

7. Find and fix the incorrect **homophone**. See pp. 36–37.

4

USING A RUBRIC TO SCORE SUMMARIES

This rubric is based on a point scale of 1 to 4. It was used to score the summaries on pages 129–132. Use this rubric to remember what is important in summaries.

4 A score of *4* means that the writer

- connects the writing directly to the prompt.
- almost always uses the correct forms of words.
- almost always uses capitalization, punctuation, and indentation correctly.
- almost always uses clear and complete sentences.
- presents the topic at the beginning of the summary.
- includes only the most important ideas from the main passage.
- does not add new information.
- uses his or her own words, except for necessary key terms from the main passage.
- puts the ideas in the same order as they appear in the main passage.

2 A score of *2* means that the writer

- connects the writing to the prompt in a general way.
- uses some incorrect forms of words and some incorrect capitalization, punctuation, and indentation.
- uses some run-on sentences or sentence fragments.
- does not clearly present the topic.
- includes some important ideas from the main passage but may also include unimportant or incomplete details.
- may add new information or opinions.
- may copy some text from the main passage.
- uses words that reflect some of the important ideas.
- puts some ideas in an order that is different from the main passage.

3 A score of *3* means that the writer

- connects the writing to the prompt.
- usually uses the correct forms of words.
- usually uses capitalization, punctuation, and indentation correctly.
- usually uses clear and complete sentences.
- presents the topic toward the beginning of the summary.
- includes many important ideas from the main passage but may also include some unimportant ideas.
- may add some new information.
- uses his or her own words, except for some key terms from the main passage.
- puts most ideas in the same order as they appear in the main passage.

1 A score of *1* means that the writer

- does not successfully connect the writing to the prompt.
- uses many incorrect forms of words and often uses incorrect capitalization, punctuation, and indentation.
- uses several run-on sentences or sentence fragments.
- may not name the topic at all.
- includes only a few important ideas from the main passage.
- often adds new information or opinions.
- may copy text from the main passage.
- uses words that do not clearly reflect the most important ideas.
- puts many ideas in an order that is different from the main passage.

SCORING SUMMARIES

Now it's your turn to score some summaries. The four summaries on this page were written in response to this prompt.

Read the nonfiction passage "Ant Colonies" on page 135. Then write a one-paragraph summary of it.

Read each summary. Write a few comments about it. Then give it a score from 1 to 4. Think about what you've learned in this lesson as you match each summary with its correct score.

Model A

Score:

Ants that are workers. They take care of nests. They take care of Queens. They fight enemys they get plants four food. they can die when they fights. They is all females Males die to.

Comments: _____

_____

_____

_____

Model C

Score:

Colonys of ants live together. Dozens or millions of ants can live in a colony. There are Queens and males and workers. Workers are all females. They care for others. Queens lay eggs. Males mate. They die young Ants work well together.

Comments: _____

_____

_____

_____

Model B

Score:

Ants are tiny insects that live in colonies. Three types of ants live in a colony. The queen lays eggs her whole life. The males mate with the queen and then die. The workers take care of the colony. Some workers also defend the colony from enemys.

Comments: _____

_____

_____

Model D

Score:

Ants live in groups called colonys. Queens and males and workers is the three kinds of ants. Ants are small insects they live in most parts of the world, but not cold places. ants like warm places. Queens live longest males dies young. Workers do most of the work.

Comments: _____

_____

_____

Here is the reading passage from which the summaries on page 134 were written.

Ant Colonies

Ants are small insects that live in most parts of the world, except in very cold areas. Ants are especially fond of warm climates.

Ants are social insects and live together in groups called *colonies*. An ant colony can have dozens of ants or millions of ants! In a colony, there are three main types of ants: queens, males, and workers. Each type of ant has its own job.

Queens Each ant colony has one or more queens. The job of a queen is to mate once with male ants. Then she lays eggs for the rest of her life. And she can live for 10 to 20 years! During her life, the queen stays safe, deep within the nest. She is fed and cleaned and cared for by other ants in the colony.

Males The male ants in a colony don't do any work to maintain the colony. They have one job and one job only. They mate with young queens. Male ants live for only a few months. They die soon after mating with the queens.

Workers The worker ants in a colony are all females. Workers live for one to five years and do most of the work in the colony. They repair the nest as needed. They may even make it larger. Workers go out and get plant food, seeds, and even other insects to feed the colony. Workers take care of the queen and her eggs. They clean and feed the developing young until they turn into adult ants. One type of worker ant, called the *soldier ant*, protects the colony. Soldiers are larger than other worker ants. They sting, bite, rip, or tear enemies. Soldier ants will often fight to the death to keep the colony safe.

WRITING A SUMMARY

Now you get to write your own summary. Use the prompt below.

> *Write a summary of the nonfiction passage "The Wolf Pack" on page 137.*

When You Write Your Summary

1. **Think about** what you want to write. As you read the longer passage, take notes on the most important ideas. (If the passage was fiction, you would take notes on the most important characters and events.)

   Use graphic organizers to gather the most important ideas.

2. **Write** your first draft. Plan a summary that will be one paragraph long. At the beginning, mention the topic of the summary. Write the most important ideas in the same order as they appear in the main reading passage. You can use key terms from the passage, but don't copy. Use your own words whenever possible. Write plainly. Avoid adding new ideas.

3. **Read** your draft. Use the checklist that your teacher will give you to review your writing.

4. **Edit** your summary. Make changes until your summary is brief and clear.

5. **Proofread** your summary one last time.

6. **Write** a neat copy of your summary and give it to your partner.

Work with a Partner

7. **Read** your partner's summary.

8. **Score** your partner's summary from 1 to 4, using the rubric on page 133. Then complete the Partner Comments sheet that your teacher will give you. Tell what you liked about the summary and what you think would make it better.

9. **Switch** papers.

10. **Think about** your partner's comments. Read your summary again. Make any changes that you think will improve your summary.

11. **Write** a neat final copy of your summary.

Making Connections

- Remember what you've learned about writing summaries when you do research for reports in social studies or science or when you write book reports.

- Pay attention to movie or book reviews that you read or hear. They often include summaries. Do they give the most important points?

- When you read magazine articles, look for headings in bold type. These will lead you to the most important ideas in the article. If there are pictures, they will relate to the most important ideas in the article.

- Many jobs require people to write summaries of very long reports and articles. What you learn about writing summaries now can also help you later in life.

Read the passage. Then follow the prompt on page 136 for writing a summary.

The Wolf Pack

Wolves are wild animals that look something like dogs, to whom they are related. Though wolves are wild, they are very social animals. Wolves live and hunt together in groups called *packs*.

Every wolf pack is built around an **order** of importance. This order helps keep peace in the pack so that the wolves can hunt and survive. Wolves go through certain actions that take the place of fighting. To show their importance, top wolves stand tall. They keep their tail up and their teeth bared. Lower wolves put their tail between their legs and often lie down. This prevents any fighting within the pack.

At the top of a wolf pack are the **alpha** male and the alpha female. These two wolves are usually the largest and strongest wolves in the pack. They are usually the ones that mate and produce pups. The alphas are also the first to eat after the pack has hunted. Next in order are the **beta** male and beta female. These two wolves are not as large or strong as the alpha pair, but they are larger and stronger than the other wolves in the pack. At the bottom of the pack order are the **omega** wolves. These poor animals are often so picked on that they leave the pack. They may become "lone wolves," who search for mates or other packs.

Though wolf **pups** aren't part of the adult order, they are very important in pack life. Wolf litters often consist of three or four pups. The pups are usually born in a den in the spring. At birth they weigh about one pound and are completely blind. The helpless pups stay with their mother, who nurses them. Other wolves in the pack bring the mother food while she is nursing the

pups. In a few weeks, the pups can open their eyes. Then they begin to walk around the den. The pack stays around the den as the pups grow. In about a year, the pups are big enough to join the pack. As adult wolves, they will challenge other adults to find their order in the pack.

Writing to give information is called **expository** writing. When you see test prompts for expository writing, you must use facts and examples that you already know. In school, however, you are asked to write reports about real people, places, or things. For these reports, you have to search out the facts and examples. Here are some tips on writing **research reports.**

TOPIC

Your teacher will sometimes give you a specific **topic** for your report. At other times, your teacher will give only a general subject. Then you will have to narrow the subject to a more specific topic. That way, you can write a clearly focused report.

If you have a subject such as "animals" to write about, you can narrow the topic by asking yourself questions. For example: Do I want to write about

- pet animals?
- small animals?
- furry animals?
- animals in the wild?

If you choose animals in the wild, which wild animals do you want to write about? Wolves? Lions? Elephants?

You should choose an animal in which you have an interest and about which you can gather specific details.

If you decide to write about elephants, think of a question that you want your report to answer. This will be the topic.

- Where do elephants live?
- What do elephants look like?
- What do elephants eat?

If you choose what elephants look like as your topic, ask more questions.

- What is an elephant's trunk like?
- What are an elephant's teeth like?
- What are an elephant's ears like?

SOURCES

Once you have narrowed the topic, find **sources** for information. You might use nonfiction books, encyclopedias, magazine articles, and the Internet.

NOTES

Once you have found a few good sources, take **notes** on your topic. You can use graphic organizers. You can also write short notes on index cards or in a notebook.

At last, it's time to organize your notes for your report. An **outline** is one of the best ways to organize information for a report.

Here's how to create an **outline** for your report. First, write the **topic** of the report at the top. Next, list each question that you want to answer. Turn each question into an idea. Under each **main idea**, write at least two **details**. Follow this outline style.

report topic	**What an Elephant Looks Like**
main idea 1	I. **An elephant's trunk**
detail 1	A. _____
detail 2	B. _____
detail 3	C. _____
main idea 2	II. **An elephant's teeth**
detail 1	A. _____
detail 2	B. _____
detail 3	C. _____
main idea 3	III. **An elephant's ears**
detail 1	A. _____
detail 2	B. _____
detail 3	C. _____

Look at the report on page 140. The writer probably used the outline above. Use the report to fill in the details on this outline.

A **report** should include the main ideas and details from your outline. These make up the **body** of the report. A report should also include a short **opening paragraph** and **closing paragraph**. A final report should have three main parts.

Beginning A strong **title** that grabs readers' attention and a short **opening paragraph** that introduces the topic.

Middle **Main ideas** and **supporting details** that make up the body of the report.

Ending A **closing paragraph** that sums up the ideas in the report.

Here's a report about what elephants look like. The writer used the outline on page 139 to write a draft. Then the writer edited and proofread the report. The final report scored a 4. It will be published in a class book.

A Unique Animal

Beginning

What animal has a long nose that is sometimes used like an arm? Why, it's the elephant! Elephants are huge land animals that live mostly in Africa and Asia.

Middle

One of the most interesting things about an elephant is its trunk. An elephant's trunk is like a nose and an arm in one. An elephant uses its trunk to breathe and to smell. The trunk can pick up food and suck up water. This is important because an elephant needs about 300 pounds of food and 40 gallons of water each day! An elephant also uses its trunk to spray water, pat friends, and make loud noises. An elephant's trunk is both strong and sensitive. It can lift up a tree trunk or a peanut.

Elephants have flat teeth for grinding up all the grasses, barks, and other foods they eat. They also have two very long teeth called tusks. Tusks can be used for digging deep in the earth for roots or buried water. Tusks can strip bark off trees. Elephants may also use their huge tusks for fighting.

An elephant's ears can measure five feet from top to bottom. Those are big ears! Elephants use their ears for hearing and also for cooling. In the heat, an elephant flaps its ears around. The air cools the blood that is flowing through the ears. The blood then flows through the rest of the elephant and cools it off.

Ending

Elephants are not just huge. They also have unique looks!

PREPARE FOR A TEST

On pages 141–143 are some writing prompts that you might see on tests. Follow each prompt and use the tips provided.

Prompt 1: Write a description of your best friend.

Tips

▲ Read the prompt carefully.

▲ Think about your friend. Choose the most interesting details about your friend. How does your friend look, talk, and act? What does your friend like and dislike?

▲ Remember to use a graphic organizer to gather and sort sense words and details.

▲ State at the beginning that you are describing your best friend.

▲ Use strong, colorful words to make your description come alive for readers.

▲ Use comparisons to add to the description.

▲ Read through your description. Make sure it creates a strong image of your friend.

▲ Make sure you indent your description.

▲ Check your description for correct capitalization, punctuation, and word use.

Prompt 2: Write a story about a time when you found something unusual.

Tips

▲ Read the prompt carefully.

▲ Think about what happens in the story.

▲ Make sure the story is about your own life. Use the word *I* in the story.

▲ Name the other characters in the story. Tell when and where the story takes place.

▲ Remember to use a graphic organizer to arrange the main story parts and events.

▲ Plan a clear beginning, middle, and ending.

▲ Tell the events in an order that makes sense.

▲ Use exact words and various kinds of sentences.

▲ Begin a new paragraph for each new idea. Indent each paragraph.

▲ Read through your story to be sure it flows.

▲ Check your story for correct capitalization, punctuation, and word use.

▲ Think of an interesting title that tells something about the story.

Prompt 3: Use your imagination to write a story about someone making a big mistake.

Tips

▲ Read the prompt carefully.

▲ Think carefully about the events in the story.

▲ Decide on the main character and the other characters in the story.

▲ Decide when and where the story takes place.

▲ Think about what problem the characters must deal with.

▲ Decide what the characters will do to correct the problem and what the result is.

▲ Remember to use a graphic organizer to arrange the main story parts and events.

▲ Plan a clear beginning, middle, and ending.

▲ Use exact words and various kinds of sentences.

▲ Try to have characters talk with one another. Begin a new paragraph for each different speaker. Indent each new paragraph.

▲ Read through your story to be sure it flows.

▲ Check your story for correct capitalization, punctuation, and word use.

▲ Think of a title for the story that will catch readers' interest.

Prompt 4: Name your favorite school subject and write an essay that explains why it is your favorite.

Tips

▲ Read the prompt carefully.

▲ Think about how you will present your explanation.

▲ Remember to use a graphic organizer to arrange main ideas and details.

▲ State the topic clearly at the beginning.

▲ Be sure that each paragraph in the middle states an important point about the topic. Include facts and examples as supporting details. Indent each paragraph.

▲ Present the ideas in an order that makes sense.

▲ Use clear, exact words and various kinds of sentences.

▲ Write a strong ending that ties up the main points of the essay.

▲ Read through your essay. Be sure it explains why that school subject is your favorite.

▲ Check your essay for correct capitalization, punctuation, and word use.

▲ Think of a title that tells clearly what the essay is about.

Prompt 5: *Write an opinion about a rule at school or at home.*

Tips

▲ Read the prompt carefully.

▲ Think about your opinion on the topic and the reasons for that opinion.

▲ Remember to use a graphic organizer to gather and sort reasons and facts.

▲ Plan a beginning, middle, and ending.

▲ Introduce the topic and your opinion at the beginning.

▲ Provide strong reasons to support your opinion. Back up your reasons with facts and examples.

▲ Begin a new paragraph for each new idea. Indent each new paragraph.

▲ Present your reasons in an order that makes the opinion stronger.

▲ Use clear and effective words and a variety of sentences.

▲ Write a strong ending that states one of your strongest reasons or facts.

▲ Read through your opinion to be sure it is strong and clear.

▲ Check your opinion for correct capitalization, punctuation, and word use.

▲ Think of a title that states your opinion clearly.

Prompt 6: *Write a one-paragraph summary of the passage "Tarantulas" on page 144.*

Tips

▲ Read the prompt carefully.

▲ Read the passage on page 144. Look for the most important points.

▲ Remember to use a graphic organizer to sort out the most important ideas.

▲ Plan your summary to be one paragraph long. Indent the paragraph.

▲ State the topic at the beginning.

▲ Use your own words when you present the most important ideas. Do not copy the main passage, but you may use some key terms.

▲ Keep the summary clear and simple. Don't add new ideas or colorful language.

▲ Present the important ideas in the same order as they appear in the main passage.

▲ End the summary with the final important idea from the main passage.

▲ Read through the summary to make sure it is short and clear.

▲ Check your summary for correct capitalization, punctuation, and word use.

Read the passage. Then follow Prompt 6 on page 143.

TARANTULAS

A tarantula is a type of spider. There are many kinds of tarantulas. They live in many parts of the world. They especially like dry areas.

What They Look Like

Tarantulas have furry bodies and long legs. Tarantulas come in different colors. Many are black, brown, or gray. Some are blue. Some even have colored stripes on their legs! Whatever the color, all tarantulas have one thing in common. They have long fangs, or teeth.

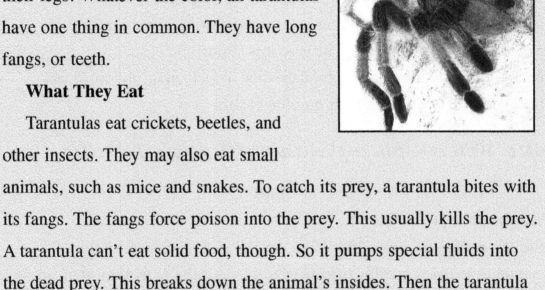

What They Eat

Tarantulas eat crickets, beetles, and other insects. They may also eat small animals, such as mice and snakes. To catch its prey, a tarantula bites with its fangs. The fangs force poison into the prey. This usually kills the prey. A tarantula can't eat solid food, though. So it pumps special fluids into the dead prey. This breaks down the animal's insides. Then the tarantula sucks up its dinner.

How They Protect Themselves

Tarantulas can live for many years if they stay safe from their enemies. Snakes, toads, birds, and wasps like to eat tarantulas. Some tarantulas shoot hairs at enemies. The hairs have many small, sharp points. These barbs stick in the other animal and sting and itch. Other tarantulas bite their enemies. A tarantula bite can kill another animal, but it will never kill a human. It can really hurt, though!